HORSE POWER

MARYLIAN WATNEY   SANDERS WATNEY

HORSE POWER

HAMLYN London · New York · Sydney · Toronto

Acknowledgements

The authors are grateful to the following people for their advice and help:
J. A. Allen Esq., Australia House, R. A. Brown Esq., O.B.E., Col. K. Capel-Cure A.F.C., R.A.S.C., The Carriage Association of America, Brigadier L. H. Crumby, W. J. Goddard Esq., Miss Daphne Machin Goodall, Imperial War Museum, India Office, Leslie Lane Esq., The Mansell Collection, Lt. Colonel J. Miller, C.V.O., D.S.O., M.C., Troop, R.H.A., National Army Museum, National Coal Board, New Zealand House, Mrs. Mary Pain, J. Pemberton Esq., Pickfords Ltd., Mrs. B. Sewell, Swiss National Tourist Board, R. A. S. Thomas Esq., United Dairies Ltd.

Photographic Acknowledgements

Colour Plates: Ardea Photographics 18–19, 79 bottom; Author 10–11; Peter Baker 70–71, 74–75; Camera Press Back jacket top; Joy Claxton 66 bottom; W. F. Davidson 50, 51; Hamlyn Group Picture Library Front jacket, 7 bottom, 14, 15, 22–23, 26–27, 66 top, 67; Mansell 62–63, 78–79 top, 78 bottom; Victoria & Albert Museum 54–55.

Black and white illustrations: Author 9, 12, 13, 21, 37 bottom, 39 top, 43 top, 45, 53 bottom, 69 bottom, 72 bottom, 73 top; Bettmann Archive 52 bottom; Commissioner of the Metropolitan Police 42 lower centre; Courtesy of H.M. Postmaster General 28, 29; Mary Evans' Picture Library 16, 20, 30–31, 32–33, 35, 37 top, 46–47, 58–59, 76–77, 82, 88 top, 93 top; Foto Tiedemann 81 bottom; Daphne Machin Goodall 80 bottom left; Imperial War Museum 56 centre & bottom, 57; India Office Library 93 bottom; Irish Tourish Board 73 bottom; Mrs. Edith La Francis 60, 61, 64, 65; V. Lahdenniemi 83 left; Leslie Lane 95; London Fire Brigade 42 top; Jack de Lorme 68; Machatschek, Paris 52 top; Mansell Title-page, 6, 7, 40–41, 56 top, 72 top, 80–81, 83 right, 84–85, 88 bottom, 90–91; Werner Menzendorf 80 top left; Mustograph 44; Museum of British Transport, Back jacket bottom right; National Coal Board 43 bottom, back jacket bottom left; Popperfoto 86, 87, 89, 92; Radio Times Hulton Picture Library 24–25, 34, 36, 38, 39 bottom, 42 upper centre, 42 bottom; Hugh Sibley 49 bottom; H. Sting 81 top right; John Tarlton 48 top; John Topham 48 bottom, 49 top, 53 top; Topix 94; United States Information Service 69.

The publishers are grateful to the Curator of Dodington Carriage Museum for allowing items from the collection to be photographed, for this publication.

Bibliography

Annals of the Road by Capt. Malet, *Longmans Green* 1876
Down the Road by C. Birch Reynardson, *Longmans Green* 1876
Highways and Horses by Athol Maudslay, *Chapman & Hall* 1888
The Horse World of London by W. J. Gordon, 1893 (Re-issued *J. A. Allen & Co.* 1972)
Omnibuses & Cars by H. C. Moore, *Chapman & Hall* 1902
Manual of Horsemastership & Animal Transport, HMSO. 1937
The English Carriage by Hugh McCausland, *Batchworth* 1948
The Horse in the Furrow by G. Ewart Evans, *Faber & Faber* 1960
The Morgan Horse by Jeanne Mellin, *S. Greene (USA)* 1961
The Elegant Carriage by M. Watney, *J. A. Allen & Co.* 1961
The Royal Mews, *Pitkin Pictorial Guides* 1964
Horses of the World by Daphne Machin Goodall, *Country Life* 1965

The Pattern Under the Plough by G. Ewart Evans, *Faber & Faber* 1966
The Lights of Cobb & Co. by K. A. Austin, *Angus & Robertson* 1966
Buses Trolleys & Trams by Chas. Dunbar, *Hamlyn* 1967
On the Box Seat by Tom Ryder, *Horse Drawn Carriages* 1969
The History of the Carriage by Laszlo Tarr, *Vision Press* 1969
19th Century Horses & Carriages, *Perpetua Press* 1971
Transport in Australia by Max Colwell, *Hamlyn* 1972
The Heavy Horse—Its Harness & Decoration by Terry Keegan, *Keegan* 1973
Travel & Transport in Ireland, *Macmillan & Gill* 1973
The Carriage Journal—quarterly magazine, *The Carriage Association in the USA.*

Published by the Hamlyn Publishing Group Limited
London · New York · Sydney · Toronto
Astronaut House, Feltham, Middlesex, England.
Copyright © The Hamlyn Publishing Group Limited 1975

ISBN 0 600 34419 3

Printed in Czechoslovakia by Polygrafia, Prague
51670

Contents

Remarkably, it is not known who invented the wheel, which even today must be regarded as the greatest invention of all time. Most probably it was evolved from the crude wooden rollers which the Egyptians used in the construction of the Pyramids. Earlier and more primitive civilizations had made rough sledges which were man-handled, and eventually pulled by domestic animals. These, curiously, lasted for many years, particularly in Ireland where they were known as 'slide-cars'.

Chariots, drawn by two horses, which had wheels containing spokes—obviously a later development—are said to have been used by the Syrians as early as 1600 BC, while the Persians are reported as having fastened scythes to the hubs of their wheels in order to plough through their enemies' ranks. This practice was later adopted elsewhere, and is alleged to have been used by Queen Boadicea. Chariots with four wheels were tried by both the Greeks and the Romans, although they were not found to be successful. They therefore reverted to those with two wheels, but since these had no springs—the floor of

the chariot being directly supported on the axle—they must have been extremely uncomfortable to ride in and it is difficult to imagine how they could have been successfully driven at speed over rough ground. Perhaps it was for this reason that chariots were used exclusively for war or the sport of chariot racing, and never developed for transport.

Although the Romans left good roads in England, these were not kept in repair so that wheeled travel in the country soon became virtually impossible, and the only means of communication was by pack-horse, or for those who could not ride, by litters strapped to two horses in tandem. Large wagons, however, were eventually built, and in a vain attempt at improving the road surfaces were placed on rollers instead of wheels, but even these vehicles could only run in summer.

The building of coaches and carriages for use in towns continued and the first of many traffic jams is recorded by the proclamation issued in 1650 which forbade the use of coaches in London, *"except for travelling five miles out of same."* Hungary is the country reported as having been

6

Left: Harnessing a chariot in ancient Greece. The illustration is part of the decoration on a 'black figure' amphora of the 6th Century BC, which has been 'unrolled' to give an undistorted view.
Top: A procession of gypsies, by Jacques Callot (1592–1635).
Above: The glorious days of coaching, recaptured.

the chief instigators in coach-building, and were the first to use leather straps for supporting the body of a coach on posts. These were later to be replaced by C-springs. Springs made of steel did not make their appearance until 1700, and it was not until many years later that the elliptical spring was invented. This, together with the improvement in road surfaces, led to further developments in carriage building and to the full use of *horse power*.

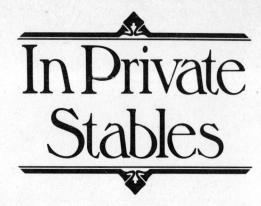

In Private Stables

OME OF THE EARLIEST CARRIages were large and very clumsily built and at this period roads were extremely bad. Smaller and roughly made gigs were available, which consisted merely of wooden boards fixed above the shafts, for if they cost less than £12 and had the words 'Taxed Cart' painted on them the amount levied was only twelve shillings a year—as compared with a charge of over £3 on all other two-wheeled vehicles. On account of this high taxation, most vehicles were hired from coach factories, but later the Government was forced to repeal this Act, and consequently carriages began again to be bought in large numbers.

With the improvement in road surfaces, many vehicles of differing design came into being, and from the late 18th Century onwards, when young men, headed by the Prince Regent, took to driving four-in-hands, the fashion for driving as a sport began, with the horse and carriage becoming a prized possession, whereas it had formerly been merely a means of conveyance. The year 1794 saw the publication of the first book on coach-building, by William Felton, and the drawings in this reveal the elegance in design which was soon to make England famous for its carriages.

The earliest vehicles of this type to be owner-driven were the high Phaetons, which consisted of two varieties: The High Perch, which was built with a single 'perch' undercarriage like that of a Mail Coach; and the Crane-Neck, which was built on two hooped iron cranes, under which the front wheels could turn, thus making the vehicle considerably more wieldy. On account of their height, both these varieties were colloquially known as "Highflyers" and it is thought that the name phaeton was derived from the legendary son of Helios, who drove his father's sun-chariot, lost control of the horses and crashed through the clouds, thereby nearly setting the earth on fire. Highflyer phaetons could be drawn by a pair, four, or six horses, and according to contemporary paintings only the pair in the wheel were driven from the box—the others being postillion driven. This, of course, might have been dangerous should a postillion-rider become dislodged, and so an emergency device worked by foot from the box-seat, which opened the hook on the end of the pole—thus releasing the leading horses—was invented as a safety precaution.

Other high vehicles were the Tandem Cart; the Suicide Gig, which was reported as having the groom's seat at the back, built three feet above that of the driver; and the Cocking Cart, which, with its slatted sides inserted into the boot under the seat, provided ventilation when transporting fighting cocks, and was the forerunner of another carriage to be built later with the same idea for carrying sporting dogs.

After the extreme heights of some of the early vehicles, two much lower ones were imported from abroad: the first was the Curricle, which originated in Italy; and the second the Cabriolet from France. Both vehicles became immensely fashionable for gentlemen to drive, and it is reported that the Curricle in particular was much favoured by the Prince Regent, the Duke of Wellington, the Marquis of Anglesey, and by Count d'Orsay. Both carriages were two-wheeled, but while the Cabriolet was built like all two-wheeled vehicles, with shafts for a single horse, the Curricle was unusual in that it had a pole for a pair, the weight being supported by a steel bar fitted to the pads across the horses' backs. Since Curricles were extremely fast on the road, they became popular for driving both in and out of towns, as well as for road matches and wagers of speed. In addition to being drawn by a pair, 'Unicorn' teams, consisting of one leader in front of a pair, were occasionally put to them. Cabriolets, on the other hand, were strictly speaking, town vehicles, and it became a fashion to have a very large quality horse, with a tiny groom who stood on a platform at the back and who became known as a 'tiger', because it was traditional for his livery to include a yellow-and-black striped waistcoat. Another innovation on Cabriolets was the hanging of a bell on the horse's collar—an idea which was copied very much later on Hansom Cabs. The Cabriolet itself was the original model for the first designs of small vehicle for hire on the street.

It is said that the earliest low pony phaeton was one built for George IV when he became too portly to climb into anything higher, and after this, many similarly designed vehicles were produced and became very popular, especially with ladies. In 1828 one was made for Princess Victoria to be drawn by ponies driven postillion, and later, in 1851, when she was Queen, another and even smaller phaeton—the front wheels of which were only eighteen inches high—was built and given to her by a Mr. Andrews when he was Mayor of Southampton. Some authorities state that the Queen was so pleased with this little carriage that she allowed all others like it to be

Top: A Highflyer Phaeton which was designed to include a safety device whereby the pole-hook could be opened and the leaders released in the event of the postillion rider falling off.

Above: The Curricle—a fashionable vehicle of the Regency Period and the only British two-wheeled vehicle drawn by a pair of horses.

Left: A Basket Phaeton—a vehicle built to carry ladies and children.

9

called 'Victorias', though in later years it was the bigger, box-seat driven vehicle which received this name. It is certain, however, that Queen Victoria frequently drove herself in this type of small phaeton, at Osborne and many other places, until she was quite an old lady.

Meanwhile, other and varied designs of phaetons had made their appearance, each built for a specific need or purpose. The massive Mail Phaeton, so named because it was built with the perch undercarriage of a Mail Coach, was used by men for driving in the country, exercising coach horses and even at times for travelling by post. Slightly lighter varieties of this vehicle, but without the perch undercarriage, were known as Semi or Demi-Mail Phaetons, while smaller and more elegant models with stick-back bodies were called Stanhope Phaetons, after their designer, the Hon. Fitzroy Stanhope.

Apart from the low pony phaetons, ladies, as well as gentlemen, drove elegant 'Spider' phaetons—so named because of the delicate lines of their iron-work. Another and similar carriage was the T-Cart which, like the Spider phaeton, had only a single seat at the rear for a groom, so that when viewed from the top it was shaped like a T. However, Spider phaetons, because of their elegant lines, soon replaced them. 'Siamese' was yet another name given to a variety of phaeton, and so named because unlike most of these vehicles which had smaller seats for grooms at the back, these were built with identical twin seats, one behind the other.

The 'Basket' phaeton was, as its name suggests, built with a body made of basket work, and although not very elegant it was considered before the advent of the Governess Car to be useful for transporting children, since there was no paintwork to be damaged by little enquiring fingers! So many designs of phaeton with slight differ-

A very attractive and neatly turned-out Ladies Phaeton, which was constructed with the dashboard built high, so as to hide the horses' posteriors from the driver.

ences in their construction were built at this time, and such a wide variety of names evolved for them, that even *then* it is reported to have been confusing.

After their low beginning, Gigs became very fashionable, and were built in large quantities from many different designs. Being two-wheeled, they were found to be considerably more wieldly than phaetons. Also, they required but a single horse to pull them, and they were used by a very large proportion of the population. Commercial travellers, for instance, found that the space in the boot under the seat was ideal for storing their wares, while doctors similarly discovered them useful little vehicles in which to visit their patients in the country, since they could drive themselves, tie the horse up when necessary and transport medical equipment with ease and in safety.

Of the many types of gig, the 'Stanhope', made, like

the phaeton of the same name, for the Hon. Fitzroy Stanhope, became one of the most popular as it was not only very elegant in shape—with a small spindle-backed body—but it had good springing and was therefore an extremely comfortable little carriage in which to ride. The Dennett was another variety of gig with rather a curious story concerning its name, for although it was said to have been built by a coachbuilder called Bennett, it was apparently named after three dancers, the Misses Dennett, on account of its triple springing at the back! Another fashionable gig was the 'Tilbury', which was built by a well-known coachbuilder of that name. It was unusual in that it did not possess a boot under the seat,

speed as well as over long distances, and in later years for harness racing.

For driving in the country there were small carts, and these, like gigs and phaetons, were made in a great profusion of shapes, with a correspondingly large number of names. First of these was the Dog-cart, which was designed primarily for the transport of sporting dogs and was built with a large boot under the seat in which slats were inserted to provide ventilation. One of the chief features of the Dog-cart was that unlike the gig, which never held more than two people, Dog-carts had wider seats with the back made to let down as a foot-board, so that it was possible to carry four passengers, sitting back to back. On account of their accommodation and usefulness for all types of transport, Dog-carts became so popular that they lasted until well into the motor age and were built in a great many sizes and shapes, with four as well as two wheels.

Variations on the Dog-cart consisted of the 'Eridge', designed for the Marquess of Abergavenny; the 'White-chapel', which had open railed sides and although basically a dealer's cart, was frequently used for tandem driving; and 'Spring' carts, which were similar, but had virtually no dashboards. One particularly attractive dog-cart which was designed for ladies was the 'Alexandra'—made, so it is said, for King Edward VII's Queen-Consort, who was an accomplished whip. The body of this carriage was shaped like a half-moon, with downward curving mudguards over the wheels to protect long skirts. Variations on this design were called 'Moray', 'Malvern', 'Bedford' and 'Battlesden'.

Another vehicle which sprang from the original dog-cart was the 'Ralli', which was named after a member of a well-known family from Greece who lived at Ashstead Park in Surrey. The body of this was slung lower by having the shafts inside, instead of under the vehicle, and the body curved outwards over the wheels.

Of all the little pony carriages built at this time there was one which became so useful for families that it remained in people's memories for many years. This was the Governess, or Tub cart, which was designed, as its name suggests, for the transport of children. Square in shape and low on the ground, it was entered by a little door at the back, so that once in, the occupants were not in danger of falling out—which could happen in most other carriages. It was, however, essential to have a quiet and well-behaved pony pulling it, as once in, the Governess,

but the body was hung on seven springs, which made it extremely comfortable to travel in over rough roads, though it is reported as having been a rather heavy vehicle. 'Lawton' and 'Liverpool' were two more varieties of gigs named after their builder and the town in which they were made.

Although Buggies are associated mostly with American vehicles which had four wheels of similar size, it has been recorded that this word was also used when referring to a hooded gig. In general, however, it is believed to have been the name for carriages of particularly light construction. Another light vehicle was the 'Whiskey'—so called because when in transit it was described as *"whisking along."*

'Sulkies' were also lightly built carriages, the earliest ones being made with the seat hung well above two enormously high wheels. The name 'Sulky' was evolved on account of their single and therefore solitary seats, and these were the vehicles used for road matches of both

or whoever was driving it, would have found it rather difficult to get out of in a hurry to reach the pony's head. Being essentially country vehicles, Governess carts were often made in varnished wood and with spindle panels, but some were painted, and although primarily designed to be drawn by ponies a few were made in larger sizes.

Another vehicle not unlike the Governess cart in construction was the Float. This was also enclosed and entered by a door at the back, but it was very much larger and was often used by farmers for transporting produce or small livestock to market, as well as for the delivery of milk. Since Floats could be pulled by a horse or strong cob, they were found to be useful for family outings and picnics, and although basically farm vehicles, they became extremely popular and were driven by members of the Royal family at Sandringham.

The Wagonette was another and altogether bigger type of carriage made specifically for family excursions in the country. It consisted of a body not unlike that of a Governess cart, but built with four wheels and to be driven from a box-seat. These vehicles became very fashionable and are recorded as having been built for the Duke of Portland, the Earls of both Chesterfield and Lonsdale, and eventually, in 1845, for Queen Victoria. The vogue for wagonettes soon led to the building of even larger carriages of this type, and the first 'Char-à-banc' arrived as a gift to Queen Victoria from King Louis-Philippe of France. Although the name 'Char-à-banc' (meaning a carriage with bench seats) persisted

Above: A Buggy driven by a lady.
Right: The Brougham—a coachman-driven carriage built to the design of The Chancellor, Lord Brougham, and copied extensively for use as street cars. A larger version was also made, pulled by a pair of horses and known as the 'Clarence', which when turned into a street cab received the nick-name 'Growler'. An even larger and very ornate model was called the 'Sovereign'.

for a great many years, some very similar vehicles were known as 'brakes'—sometimes spelt 'breaks'. Of these, there were several variations, the best known being the 'Body' brake, which was virtually a much longer version of the wagonette and used for such tasks as carrying large households or school-children on outings. The 'Built-up' brake, with less seating accommodation but more room for storage, and the 'Shooting' brake which, as its name suggests, was used for the pursuit of game, were other variations on the brake.

Some shooting brakes contained seats which could only be reached by the lifting up of either the front or back seats, thus imprisoning the passengers in between, and it is believed that this is how the word trap—used colloquially for horse-drawn vehicles—came into being.

Yet another type of brake was the 'skeleton', which consisted of a box-seat mounted above a low platform, and was used in both private stables and dealers' yards for breaking horses to harness—the novice having first been driven in long reins from the ground, was hitched alongside an experienced and trusted harness horse in order to accustom it to the feel and noise of a vehicle

behind, while the low platform of the vehicle was ideal for helpers to jump on and off easily, if their assistance was required.

Because carriages for private use were made in different sizes and shapes for varying and specific purposes, it followed that the animals used for drawing them also varied in height, breed and temperament. For town work, it was considered smart to have showy, high-stepping horses and ponies—a number being pure or half-bred Hackneys—while for country and long distance drives fast trotting cobs of the now extinct 'Norfolk Roadster' type were popular and many of these won wagers for their owners by performing incredible feats of speed and endurance. For small vehicles, ponies of Welsh, Dartmoor, New Forest and Shetland extraction were used, while for the larger and rustic carts the more stocky and stronger ponies such as Highland, Dales, Fells, Exmoors and Welsh cobs were found suitable.

Although driving was a necessity for most people, it was regarded as an art, and although bearing reins and severe bits were frequently used by ladies or by elderly people who experienced difficulty in controlling their horses, it was the ambition of the majority of people to be considered good whips. The fashion for driving stemmed from the late 18th Century, when young men took to four-in-hands, but different methods of harnessing were also tried: 'Unicorn' (or 'Spike' as it was sometimes called), which consisted of putting one leader in front of a pair of wheelers—a way of dealing with a four-in-hand team should a horse go lame, or sick—was one. Another was 'Pick-axe', which was harnessing in reverse—with *three* leaders in front of two wheelers, or else a pair of leaders in front of a single horse. These latter two methods never became very popular, although the name 'Pickaxe' was often and confusingly used when referring to a team driven 'Unicorn' style.

Driving horses one in front of the other in 'tandem', believed to have originated from the days when people drove to meets of hounds when the leader would eventually be mounted and ridden, was always popular with young bloods, as this, together with unicorn, were considered the two most difficult ways of driving.

'Random' (sometimes spelled 'randem'), which consisted of three horses one in front of each other, was even more daring, and although the Prince Regent is believed to have driven all the way from London to Brighton by this method, it never appears to have become sufficiently widespread to have been either depicted or reported by artists and writers of the day.

'Trandem'—the name for three horses harnessed abreast—differed from the Russian 'Troika' method, in that the horses moved at an even pace together, but it was really only used for the Shillibear omnibuses, or for work on the land.

Teams of six had been used on some of the early 'Highflyer' phaetons, where the first two pairs were invariably driven by postillion riders. It was therefore inevitable that after the passion for four-in-hands, the driving of six horses was also tried, but for some reason was never considered to have been very gentlemanly, and since it looked rather unwieldy, never became particularly popular.

Four-in-hand driving, however, had the rather extraordinary effect of producing its own vehicle, which was to retain popularity for a great many years, and is still in use today. This was the Private coach, or 'Drag', which was largely built on the lines of a Mail coach—the chief difference being in the space at the rear for two grooms, in place of the Guard's solitary seat, and with a bench for four passengers to sit opposite. Also, whereas Mail coaches were always turned out in Royal colours of maroon panels, with scarlet wheels, the Private Drag was painted in its owner's usually rather sombre family colours, with his crest or monogram painted on the door panels on either side and the boot at the back. Although private coaches such as these had no real reason for being on the highway, they were found to be useful as grandstands and were driven to such events as race-meetings and meets of the Four-in-Hand and Coaching Clubs.

While there were many vehicles built with box-seats, such as Wagonettes and Brakes, which were driven by their owners as well as by professional coachmen, there were several larger and more imposing carriages which were intended for professional drivers only. The Town

coach of early Georgian days was one, but like many vehicles of this period was large and clumsily built and required to be drawn by as many as six horses. Soon after this, Landaus, with folding hoods—so that they could be used open or shut—were imported from Germany and proved so popular that they were copied by many of the best coachbuilders. Although of a basic design in that they had four wheels and held four people, they were made in two different patterns: the 'Shelburne', or square Landau, which was said to have been designed for Lord Shelburne; and the 'Sefton', or canoe-shaped Landau, whose body resembled that of a Barouche, and was made for Lord Sefton. Since Landaus held people sitting opposite one another, they were frequently known as 'Sociables', and even as 'Vis-à-Vis'—which was originally the name for a rather similar but much more narrow carriage which was made in France. The next vehicle of this type was the Barouche, which was said to have originally been a large clumsy carriage, but which in later years was not unlike the Sefton Landau, although with lighter and more elegant lines. This was built on a perch undercarriage, and with only one hood to cover the seat for two at the back, so that in appearance it resembled a child's perambulator. Both Barouches and Landaus could be driven either from a box-seat or by postillion riders on the near-side horses.

Two more coachman-driven vehicles for town use were the Brougham and the Victoria, and of all carriages these were perhaps the most extensively copied and used, for private work and hire on the streets all over the world. The Brougham, a small, neat, enclosed carriage seating two, was originally made for Lord Brougham. A larger version made to be pulled by a pair of horses was known as the 'Clarence', which when turned into a street cab received the nick-name 'Growler'. Another and even larger and very ornate model was the 'Sovereign'. Victorias, which were open carriages and therefore used mostly in summer, were reported as having been copied from the French 'Milord'. They were entered by a low step and had sweeping mudguards covering the wheels as a protection for ladies' skirts. From time to time, other vehicles with slight variations were produced, such as the 'Droitska' from Russia, and the 'Pilentum'—both of which resembled Victorias—while the barouche-like 'Dioropha' had the advantage of having a removable hood which hung from the ceiling of the carriage house and could be lowered and fitted when the weather demanded it.

It was natural that the coach-houses of the wealthy contained a vast and impressive collection of carriages—all of them impeccably turned out and uniformly painted in the family's heraldic colours. Grooms were dressed in matching livery coats, the buttons made in either nickel or brass to correspond with the metal fittings on the harness which, in their turn, depended upon whether the family coat of arms contained a predominance of 'argent' or 'or'.

For noblemen, however, and for use upon State or ceremonial occasions, there were Dress Chariots and State Coaches (the former holding two passengers, while the latter had space for four). These were very ornate and decorated by coats of arms as well as crests painted on the door panels, while the coachmen's box-seats were covered by heavily embroidered and tasselled covers known as 'hammer cloths'. No explanation has been recorded for this curious term, but it is believed to have evolved from the fact that on these carriages the box-seats were made in the shape of a hammock. On these two carriages, the dress of coachmen and footmen was that of the Georgian period, comprising knee breeches, silk stockings and buckled shoes, with long, full and heavily braided coats. They also wore powdered wigs, under a tricorne hat for the coachman, while cocked hats were for the two footmen who stood on a platform at the back, armed with weighted and gilded staves for use against possible attack.

As was the case with some of the smaller and owner-driven carriages, fine upstanding horses were considered essential for private carriages. Those of the 'Cleveland Bay' breed, as well as the (now extinct) Yorkshire Coach horse, together with pure-bred high stepping Hackneys were in general use, but in addition a number of horses were bred for harness work with a mixture of both Hackney and Thoroughbred blood in their veins. Carriage horses always matched each other and looked superb—with heads held high above arched and shining necks, and they trotted with an impressive amount of action.

Some of the methods used to achieve these results obviously caused them great discomfort: bearing reins fitted tightly to keep their heads both up and on a level with each other, together with severe bitting to prevent them pulling against the coachmen's hands, while the urge to move on was made acute in some cases by an unpleasant process known as 'figging'—the insertion of ginger into their anal passages. Small wonder that Anna Sewell felt compelled to expose these methods in her book "*Black Beauty*". Other practices were the nicking and docking of tails, although there were basically sound reasons for this in that it prevented the reins from becoming trapped beneath the horses' tails—a situation which could render a coachman powerless, as well as lead to kicking and therefore possible accidents.

Although the horses most used for ceremonial work were Cleveland Bays, in the Royal Stables horses were imported from Hanover in Germany and of these the most famous were undoubtedly the Creams. These were first brought over in 1714 at the time of the accession of George I, and were bred at Hampton Court until 1920, when they gradually became extinct due to inbreeding. Black Hanoverian stallions were also used, and these were eventually replaced by bays, predominantly Cleveland Bays. In place of the Creams, which had always been for the use of the Sovereign only, greys were introduced and since these were originally kept at Windsor they became known as the Windsor Greys. Bays however are

still used in the Royal Mews and apart from the English breed of Cleveland Bay, Irish horses, Dutch Gelderlanders and Oldenburgs from Germany have been imported in this colour.

Apart from ceremonial and everyday transport, private horse-drawn vehicles were extensively used for longer distances. For most journeys in England where stops could be made overnight, Travelling Chariots built on the lines of the Dress Chariot and driven either from the Box or by postillion riders were used by people who could afford them. Those belonging to members of the nobility had coats of arms emblazoned on the door panels, with a sword case incorporated into the back of the body. Luggage could be carried either on the roof or the front of the vehicle, and there were seats at the back for staff.

The taste for travel, however, particularly abroad—where the Grand Tour of Europe became fashionable—soon produced carriages in which it was possible to lie full length and spend whole nights on the road. One of these was the 'Dormeuse' from France, and the other the 'Britchka' (sometimes spelled as Briska, and even Britzcha), which was introduced into England in 1818 from Austria. A third vehicle was the 'Fourgon', which was half carriage and half van in shape, and used mainly for the transport of luggage and staff. This usually preceded the other carriages by several hours, so that suitcases could be unpacked and rooms made ready to receive the travellers. For all these vehicles, pairs or teams of horses could be hired along the road under the same system as that for coaches and Post Chaises, but it was usual, in England at any rate, for the owner's horses to be used for the first two or perhaps three stages.

Horses and carriages soon developed into status symbols, and the coach-houses of the wealthy contained as complete a range as possible—to meet with each and every contingency.

Previous Two Pages: The 'Blenheim' Oxford coach.
Below: A gentleman driving a gig—a carriage in which the driver sat over the wheels and one of the lighter vehicles in use. The space under the seat could be used for strong parcels.

The Staging System

QUEEN ELIZABETH Ist IS SAID to have attended the opening of Parliament in 1571 in a coach, and although coaches were often referred to in Cromwellian times, such coaches would only have been used in towns, for public coaches were not put on the roads until about 1658. All transport outside towns had previously been by saddle or pack-horse, while for ladies who did not ride or for the elderly and infirm there were litters carried by men, horses or mules, until eventually Stage Wagons came into being. These were huge, lumbering vehicles, made of timber and with a canvas top, and drawn by teams of four, six or eight heavy horses which were urged on by drovers walking or riding beside them. On account of the state of the roads, progress was extremely slow and with the huge weight of passengers and freight behind them they were undoubtedly very hard work for the horses.

The first Stage Coaches, which ran only in summer, were also large cumbersome vehicles, made at first to hold passengers inside only, although later a basket contraption was fitted to the back to hold extra people. Springs were not introduced until the middle of the 18th Century and it was not until 1805 that it became illegal not to fit springs under the coachman's seat—the theory being that if too comfortable, the lazy fellows would fall asleep. The coachmen themselves were frequently coarse and drunken, often in league with highwaymen and footpads, knew very little about the art of driving and were satisfied if they could flog their luckless teams through the mud to the end of the stage. The stages were long at this period—sometimes twenty to thirty miles and some coaches used the same unhappy horses over the entire journey.

Gradually, however, both the roads and the system of travel improved, until in 1706 the proprietors of the York Stage coach undertook to complete the journey to London in four days, "If God permits." By 1734, when the weather was favourable, the Edinburgh to London coach performed the journey in twelve days, while a hundred years later and during the heyday of the coaching age the same distance of 397 miles was completed in $42\frac{1}{2}$ hours.

A Stage Wagon urged on by a wagoner riding beside the horses. Early wagons were constructed with very large and wide wheels. The bad road surfaces made journeys very difficult, and progress was extremely slow and tiring for the horses. Mules were also used to haul these cumbersome vehicles.

In 1784, a theatre proprietor in Bath named John Palmer made transport history by introducing the first mail-carrying coach between London and Bristol. The mails had previously been carried by post-boys on horseback, but this system was both slow and unsatisfactory as the post-boys were most unreliable, and if not in league with highwaymen and robbers, were liable to attack from them. Palmer's new method was an immediate success and as a result he was appointed Postmaster-General. The first mail-coaches were pair-horsed, but later, teams of four horses were used on all the long distance routes, with changes of horses made every seven to ten miles, so that speeds of six to eight miles an hour could be maintained even over moderate roads. Soon after, the two great engineers Telford and Macadam were on the way to completing their work of improving the roads throughout Britain, and by 1820 these were so smooth that it was said to be impossible to find a stone the size of a pigeon's egg on the road between London and Edinburgh!

After the inauguration of the Bristol mail-coach, one was put on the road to Norwich, and this was followed by routes to Leeds, Manchester, Liverpool, Holyhead, Birmingham, Shrewsbury, Portsmouth, York and Edinburgh, until mail-coaches ran regularly to all the important towns in the country. By 1830 there were ninety *four-horse* and forty-nine *pair-horse* mail-coaches running in England. Of these, twenty-seven left London nightly—all but four of them being drawn by four horses.

The organisation of the mail-coach system was that the coaches were all the property of the Post Office, who also employed the Guard, whose main duties were the delivery and safety of the mail and keeping the coachman up to time, He was provided with a blunderbuss, a clock which was locked into a leather pouch and a horn with which to warn other road users, as well as to announce both the arrival and departure of the coach. The coach horn was always colloquially known as the "*yard of tin*," as the standard horn issued by the Post Office was made of this metal and three feet in length. Guards, however, rather prided themselves on their horn blowing, so they usually provided themselves with instruments made of brass or copper, which were more melodious in tone.

The Guard always wore the Royal livery, consisting of a scarlet coat trimmed with gold braid, and the coaches were painted in royal colours—a maroon panel on the body, with scarlet wheels and undercarriage—with the Royal cypher and its registered number painted in gold on the panels on either side.

To horse the coach, the Post Office contracted with proprietors, who usually were also the innkeepers at the big terminal public houses in London, to provide the drivers and teams of horses necessary for the journey. These proprietors generally provided their own horses for the first two or three stages out of London, and then they

Previous Two Pages: A Mail Coach, with a grey off-lead horse. Grey or odd-coloured horses were often used, since they showed up in the dark.
Right: The 'Star' road coach leaving an inn at Ludgate Hill.

24

subcontracted with other innkeepers along the route to supply teams for the other stages.

Unlike other vehicles on the highway, the mail coaches travelled free on the roads, so one of the Guard's many duties was to sound the horn to alert the tollgate keepers, who had to open the gate immediately—under pain of a 40-shilling fine. The life of a Mail coach guard was a lonely one, perched as he was on a tiny and single seat at the back, with the mails locked securely in a boot under his feet. To alleviate their boredom, many mail Guards took to playing tunes on their horns to while away the time and to amuse the passengers. Such tunes as "*Pop goes the Weasel*" could often be heard. When necessary, however, the more austere calls of "*clear the road*", "*coming by*", "*pulling up*", "*turning right*" and "*turning left*" were immediately sounded.

All the London mail-coaches set off at 8 p.m. from the General Post Office in St. Martin's-le-Grand and travelled throughout the night non-stop, except for changes of horses, until their destinations were reached. The Western bound mails, however, stopped to pick up passengers and mail in the West End of London, at the Gloucester Coffee House in Piccadilly. The early mails were timed to average 8 miles an hour, but by 1830 the speed had reached 10 to 11 miles an hour. The most famous of all mail coaches, the Devonport "*Quicksilver*" (the only mail coach, incidentally, to have received a name), once completed the 217 mile journey from London to Devonport at an average speed, which included stops, of $11\frac{1}{2}$ miles an hour.

These mail coaches, which were all built and maintained by a Mr. Vidler, of Millbank, London, had seating for four passengers inside, and at one time only one seat on top—that next to the Coachman. The Post Office soon realised, however, that three more passengers could with

ease be accommodated behind the coachman and that this would in no way interfere with the Guard, and so three further seats were added. At a charge of 2½d a mile it added considerably to their takings. The charge for an inside seat was double this amount, and so the term "*outsider*", which is still in use today, was originated. The first express letters cost 3d a mile, plus a 2/6d fee, but ordinary letters were charged at 4d for every 100 miles. These figures were greatly reduced later on. By these charges, the Post Office were able to maintain its efficiency and service to the public.

With the success of the Mail coach system, Coach proprietors soon formed the idea of putting other and larger passenger-carrying vehicles on the road. These were called Road, or Stage, coaches and they were constructed to carry twelve passengers on top and four or, in some cases, six inside. They were slower than the mail coaches

as they travelled by day and had to stop to pay road tolls, but they were far cheaper—half the price of a mail coach fare. These coaches were painted in gay colours to attract attention and had the names of the towns through which they passed painted on the panels, with pictures of some of the inn signs. All were given sporting names such as "*Rocket*", "*Wonder*", "*Telegraph*", "*Comet*", "*Reynard*" and "*Red Rover*", to which were added the names of their destinations, so that they were known as the Manchester "*Telegraph*", the Shrewsbury "*Wonder*", the Southampton "*Red Rover*", and so on. Like the mails, they carried Guards, who originally only wore the Royal Livery on occasions such as the King's birthday, but later this became their official uniform, as it added to the gaiety of the turnout and made the Guard easily recognisable.

There was great competition between rival road coach proprietors and speed was, of course, the main objective, so that racing inevitably took place between the coachmen and accidents were not uncommon. Therefore, to protect the travelling public, a law forbidding galloping was passed, but since a team was held to be at the gallop when all *four* horses were going at this pace, some crafty coach proprietors managed to keep within the law by using one horse which could trot as fast as the other three galloped, and this became known as *"the Parliamentary horse"*!

Most of the innkeepers who horsed the mails at the London end prided themselves on the quality of the horses they provided for the first few stages out of London, but the animals supplied in what was called the *"middle ground"* were often very indifferent. In the stage areas which were covered in the dark the proprietors saw little point in buying expensive horses, so as long as the coachman could flog them along to the end of the stage anything was good enough. Consequently, passengers were often nervous of what lay in store for them, and a story is told of how in reply to an enquiry about the next team, an uneasy passenger once received the not very reassuring reply that it consisted of *"three blind 'uns and a bolter"*! Blind horses were not, however, such a liability, as they appeared able to sense their way, but bolting horses were another matter.

The great hazards to the coaching industry were floods, fog and snow, and a particularly hard winter in 1835 was responsible for many upsets and delays. Contemporary paintings and written descriptions both show that some Guards performed amazing feats of endurance and courage in their efforts to get the mails through, often having to ride one of the coach horses or even to walk through deep snow drifts with the mail bags on their backs.

Above: A Mail Coach descending a hill.
Below: A Mail Coach in thick snow being helped by postillion-ridden 'cock-horses'. (A painting by C. Cooper Henderson).
Right: A road coach driving through floods with the aid of cock-horses. During the severe winter of 1835, guards and drivers displayed amazing feats of courage and endurance.

Another difficulty for coaches were steep hills. For a descent, one of the back wheels could be locked by placing a metal shoe, or skid pan, under it, but if this was on for too long the wheel became so hot that it was in danger of catching fire. For ascending hills it was not unusual for the passengers to be asked to alight and help by pushing the coach—putting their *"shoulders to the wheel"*—another expression which has lasted through the centuries. For particularly long hills, it was customary to attach one, or in some cases two extra horses in front of the leaders to help pull the load. These were called *"cock"* horses—a word probably derived from coach. Cock-horses were always ridden, but if a pair was used, then only the horse on the near-side was ridden—postillion-wise—and they were attached to the coach by a long rope which ran between the leaders to the hook on the end of the pole. Cock-horses were frequently stabled at inns situated either at the foot or top of steep hills, and these were invariably named *"The Cock"*, for this reason. The nursery rhyme *"Ride a cock-horse to Banbury Cross"* is probably accounted for by a particularly long and steep hill which exists outside Banbury, Oxfordshire.

During the coaching era a good many accidents occurred, some of them because it became fashionable for young men about town to drive four-in-hands, and although this was officially not allowed for safety reasons it has been recorded that it took place nevertheless.

One incident was so curious, however, that James Pollard, the artist, made it the subject for a painting which has since been reproduced as a print. This happened on the night of October 20th, 1816, when the *"Quicksilver"* mail-coach was approaching the *"Pheasant Inn"* at Winterslow, on Salisbury Plain. The coachman noticed his horses becoming restive, and what in the dark he took to be a calf trotting alongside them. By springing at one of the leaders, however, the animal revealed itself to be an escaped lioness, which severely mauled the unfortunate horse. Luckily, the lioness was both beaten off and recaptured, and the horse recovered from its wounds to live to a great age.

There were numerous coach proprietors involved in the exacting and complicated business of running and horsing the mail and stage coaches, and several of them at the London end were in a very big way of business. Two of the largest were William Chaplin of *"The Swan with Two Necks"* in Lad Lane, and Edward Sherman of *"The Bull and Mouth"*, St. Martins-le-Grand. Some indication of the size of the undertaking is that Chaplin owned 1,700 horses, while Sherman had over 1,000. Other proprietors were Benjamin Horne of *"The Golden Cross"*, Charing Cross; Robert Gray of *"The Bolt in Tun"*, Fleet Street; and two women Mrs. Ann Nelson of the *"Bull"* Aldgate and Mrs. Sarah Mountain of *"The Saracen's Head"*, Snow Hill. Both these ladies were widows who, with the aid of their sons, carried on their husbands' businesses and both were well known, but for different reasons: Mrs. Nelson because of her extreme kindness and consideration towards the coachmen and guards in her employ, and Mrs. Mountain for the extensive coach-building business which she ran at the rear of her premises.

Whereas travel by mail or by stage coach was relatively expensive and considered superior to the slow but cheaper journeys in stage wagons endured by poorer people, the really first-class method of travel was by Post Chaise or in a Travelling Chariot. These were virtually identical

The 'Royal Blue' road coach, said to have been so named after an
incident connected with Queen Victoria when she was riding
side-saddle in a navy-blue habit.

vehicles, the latter being a gentleman's private carriage and painted in his own colours, with his coat of arms, family crest or monogram emblazoned on the doors, while the former was merely a discarded and second-hand and therefore rather shabby version of it which could be hired by anyone with sufficient money to pay—1/6d a mile being the charge for two horses, and double that for four.

Post Chaises were always painted yellow, and were therefore nick-named "*Yellow Bounders*" and were available for hire from all better class inns, while the horses pulling them were always ridden postillion by post-boys wearing traditional yellow jackets and beaver hats. These post-boys, who frequently were elderly men, rode for stages of between seven to twelve miles, returning to their bases—unless another fare was forthcoming—at the end of the stage. The life of a post-horse, and indeed of a post-boy, was not a very happy one as they never knew how many miles or hours they would be called upon to work. This was in contrast to that of the coach-horses and coach-men, who at least had both regular hours and stages.

The vast industry of running transport throughout Britain by means of wagons, mail and stage coaches, and post-chaises, reached its height in about 1840—the roads being in first-class condition, the coaches well-horsed, expertly driven and invariably punctual. It was said that clocks were set by the arrival of the coaches. The industry was organised to such a pitch that fast trotting cobs were provided for hard, hilly stages and galloping thoroughbreds for level ground, but the railways had begun to infiltrate throughout the country and although the coach proprietors fought them for some years the collapse of coach services was inevitable, and by 1846 main line railways were available to all the major cities.

Coaches continued to run in parts of the country and out of the way villages not served by rail, but the industry as a whole was dead. The coach proprietors faced bankruptcy, and the coachmen, guards and all the many attendant workers in the industry were forced to seek other employment. Most of the guards took similar work on the railways, but the crack coachmen did not take kindly to the "*Iron Horse*", and had to sink their pride by driving omnibuses and cabs. The British roads, which had been the envy of the world, fell largely into disrepair and were not used again for nearly a hundred years, until the advent of the motorcar and its attendant industry.

Public Transport in Towns

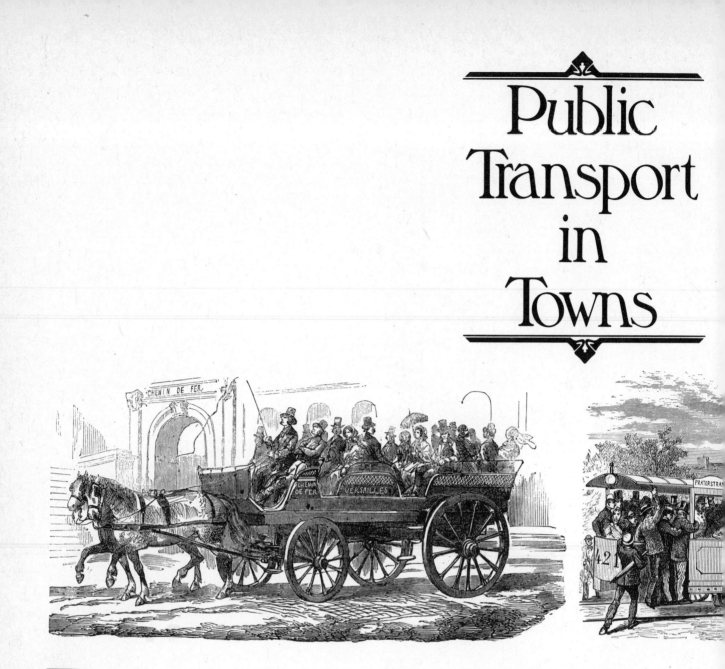

UBLIC TRANSPORT, IN THE FORM of huge, lumbering stage wagons, had been in operation throughout the country in England during the 17th Century, but it was not until very much later that passenger-carrying vehicles of any size were evolved for town-work. Hackney coaches had, it is true, been available for hire in London until the traffic jams, but these were reported as having been very small, narrow vehicles. After the Great Fire of London in 1666, when the streets were widened, Town coaches, which were the discarded carriages of noblemen and drawn by pairs of horses, were used, but these again held no more than four people and so scarcely contributed towards a vast passenger-carrying service.

It was in Paris, and as early as 1662, that the very first omnibuses are reported to have been built. These were known as "*carrosses à cinq sous*" and to begin with they caused a small furore, but since only eight passengers could be carried, Parisians soon found it almost as easy and certainly much cheaper to walk, and so the craze for them died. Larger vehicles did not make their appearance until 1819, and these, which held eighteen people, were put on the streets by a Monsieur Lafitte, who also introduced the name 'Omnibus', and their success was immediate and lasting. London did not however see its first omnibus until 1829, and this was produced by a Mr. George Shillibear, a former midshipman in the Navy who became apprenticed to Hatchett, the well-known coach-builder in Long Acre, and then left to set up his own business in Paris. It was there, while building one of Monsieur Lafitte's omnibuses, that he thought of introducing them to London, where the public promptly christened them "Shillibears", despite the fact that the word 'Omnibus' was painted in large letters on either side of the vehicle.

ing to alight on either side of the road could pull the appropriate cord. This innovation became immensely popular and was copied by a number of 'bus proprietors, among them a Mr. Wilson, whose 'Favourite' omnibuses ran from "*The Nag's Head*", Holloway, to Fulham.

At this time most omnibuses, like the Stage coaches, received distinctive names, and apart from the 'Favourites', there were, to quote a few, 'Hopes', 'Wellingtons', 'Napoleons', Marlboroughs' and 'Paragons'. One of these, the line of 'Eagles', which were always painted green, changed both its name and colour to 'Royal Blue' in deference to an incident, which has received different connotations, connected with Queen Victoria.

After various ups and downs in the trade, Shillibear finally gave up being a bus proprietor in 1838 when he tried unsuccessfully to compete with the Greenwich railway, and instead he became an undertaker, in which profession, with his meticulous attention to detail, he became very successful. His vehicles continued to be known as

Left, below: A French char-à-banc.
Below: A Viennese horse-drawn tram-car.
Right, below: A French omnibus.

The first two omnibuses were built to carry twenty-two people—all inside. Pulled by three horses harnessed abreast, they were run from "*The Yorkshire Stingo*", Paddington, to the Bank in the City, at a fare of one shilling. These performed twelve trips a day and became very popular, since Shillibear not only provided free newspapers and magazines, but his conductors, who were the sons of Naval friends and wore smart blue uniforms cut like those of a midshipman, became known for their charm and good manners, and within nine months the number of omnibuses rose to twelve.

So successful was this enterprise that omnibuses of a similar design soon took the place of the short-stage coaches which had previously been the only kind of public transport available, and many rival proprietors began in opposition to Shillibear. Some of these provided different and unusual attractions: shelves full of books being produced by one, while another hit on the idea that his coachmen should wear on their arms wooden rings, to which were attached long pieces of string so that passengers wish-

Shillibears until well after his retirement from their proprietorship, although once he had established himself in undertaking, the public, not wishing to travel in anything associated with funerals, reverted to calling them 'Omnibuses'—thus preventing his name from continuing as a household word, as was the case with 'Hansom' cabs.

The next development in omnibus design was in 1851 when the 'Knifeboard' bus was introduced. This was the first to carry passengers on top as well as inside—the seating arrangement consisting of a central low plank running the length of the roof on which the passengers sat back to back and facing outward. At a much later date, two boards were fitted to the sides of the roof, so that when ladies occupied these seats there was no risk of their ankles being visible to passers-by—and these were known as modesty boards. It was not long before the publicity potential of omnibuses was realised and these boards became a useful means of displaying advertisements. Later still and during the 19th Century another design of omnibus, the 'Garden Seat', which had a double row of seats

33

in pairs, one behind the other and facing the front, was produced, and this type became so popular that it soon superseded all the other models.

The most famous of all bus proprietors and jobmasters in London was Thomas Tilling of Peckham, who began in 1847 with one horse, and by 1851 had put his first bus on the road. Before the end of the century his Company owned a stud of 4,000 horses and 160 omnibuses, and were the largest jobmasters in the world. In 1900 there were 3,700 omnibuses in London alone, and each would require ten horses to keep it on the road. The London General Omnibus Company owned 1,000 omnibuses and about 10,000 horses which, in the course of a year, travelled approximately 20,000,000 miles. Next in size was the Road Car Company with 450 buses and 5,200 horses, and there were also a number of smaller companies. All the major companies worked on recognised routes within the framework of an association, but some of the smaller operators ran rival 'pirate' buses on unauthorised routes, in an endeavour to steal passengers from the regulars. Both parties resorted to every sort of trick, and as the Association companies did not mind making a loss on one or two buses they would try to put an unfair competitor out of business by a method of

Top: A line of 'garden-seat' omnibuses at Charing Cross, London, in the gay nineteen hundreds.
Above: A pair-horse tram at Portsmouth at the turn of the century.
Right: De Tivoli's patent 'knife-board' omnibus run by the Great Western railway.
Far right: A pair-horse railway car at Birkenhead, carrying up to seventy passengers.

'nursing'—which consisted of running a regular bus both in front and behind the rival.

Every bus, with a loaded weight of about 2½ tons, made four full trips a day, each consisting of approximately twelve miles, in an average time of 3½ hours. Each bus required a stud of ten or eleven horses. The horses were changed every trip so that eight horses a day were worked and each pair had a rest every fifth day. The eleventh horse was used as a spare, and worked into the scheme on a rota when, as sometimes happened, a short trip was added to the four daily full trips. From this it can be seen that bus horses did not work long hours, although their work was hard and the constant stopping and starting played havoc with their legs, so that they seldom lasted more than four or five years on the roads, after which they were either sent to the knacker or sold cheaply for work on the land.

As about 5,000 horses were required every year to supply the London bus companies alone, horse dealers had to travel far and wide to be able to meet the demand. Bus horses were of a cross-bred cart-horse type, usually with some hair about the legs, and they came from all over England and Ireland, as well as from Canada. Some bus companies, including the London General Omnibus Company, preferred to have mares, for which they paid about £35 each, and at least one company experimented with working horses in London unshod. To do this, they hardened their feet by trotting the remounts continually on hard roads, and on most road surfaces this was apparently a success but when it snowed the horses' feet had to be shod with frost nails.

Horses which had an even harder life than those used with buses were the ones whose lot it was to pull trams. A two-horse tram-car weighs 2¾ tons, and double this when full, so that they were required to pull two tons more than the bus horses. Although trams ran smoothly and without much effort on the level, the constant starting was a great strain and the working life of a tram-car horse has been recorded as being a year less than those which pulled the buses.

Apart from omnibuses and trams there were in the towns a great many smaller and more expensive vehicles available for hire on the streets. The word "Hackney"—which was derived from the French "Haquenée", mean-

ing a horse for hire, appeared in the English language as early as the 17th Century and was applied to coaches for hire at that time. In about 1805, some small gig-like vehicles had made their appearance and these began the desire for altogether much smaller carriages, which resulted in many and different designs being produced. The first of these to be licensed was the Hackney Cabriolet designed by Mr. David Davies, the coachbuilder in Albany Street. This was identical to the two-wheeled gentleman's Cabriolet, which was such a popular vehicle, but had in addition a driver's seat *outside*—between the body and wheels of the carriage—so that by raising the hood and drawing the curtains and leather apron across, the occupants could have a certain amount of privacy inside. In 1830 another design known as the 'Coffin' cab made its appearance. This also had the driver's seat outside the body of the vehicle, but the hood differed by being tall, narrow and box-like in shape, which accounted for the name.

Within two years, another and square-shaped cab with the driver sitting on the roof was brought out by a Mr. Boulnois. This was also two-wheeled, but had a door at the back, which soon proved a disadvantage when unscrupulous passengers found that they could escape unnoticed without paying their fares. This vehicle was known as the 'Back-door' cab, or 'Minibus'—to distinguish it from a larger variety called the 'Duobus'.

Mr. Hansom's cab did not appear until 1834, but it was not shaped anything like the vehicle which became famous and bore his name, since it was extremely large and square, with wheels said to be 7 feet 6 inches high and with the driver sitting on the *front* of the roof. Mr. Hansom is reported as having driven this vehicle to London from his home in Leicestershire and to have received an offer of £10,000 from a company willing to build and market it, but faults were soon discovered and the company withdrew to renew their offer two years later to a Mr. John Chapman, who had built the cab destined to become the most popular of all and to bear Hansom's name

Cabs built with four wheels were put on the road shortly after 'Hansoms' became popular. These held two people inside and one on the box beside the driver, and it was said that it was from these that Lord Brougham got the idea for the private carriage which eventually bore his

Above: A Hansom Cab, known as the 'Gondola of London';
a 'dashing' vehicle.
Left: A 'Growler' which accommodated all types of luggage on
the roof.
Right, above: A livery stable poster of 1893.
Right: A forerunner of the Hansom Cab—the 'Coffin Cab'.

name. It was not long before larger vehicles, built to carry
four or more people were made and these were known
as 'Clarences', but when used as cabs, were nick-named
'Growlers' on account of the noise they made when in
transit. Hansoms, which also received the title "*Gondolas
of London*" were always thought of as being rather dashing
vehicles, and respectable ladies never considered travelling in them either alone or accompanied by gentlemen
other than their husbands. Growlers, on the other hand,

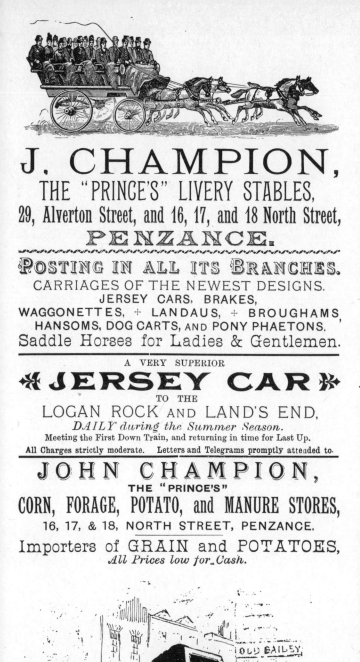
which were useful for transporting families and luggage, were regarded as necessary but dull vehicles, as indeed they probably were, and the leather upholstery inside frequently retained a peculiar and unpleasant musty smell.

Two new cabs appeared in 1844, the first being a type of Hansom called the 'Tribus' which held three people and was entered from the back with the driver's seat placed at the side so that he could open or shut the door without having to get down. These vehicles were occasionally built to take a pair of horses in curricle harness. The second was a four-wheeler which held four passengers and was known as the 'Quartobus', but neither of these cabs became popular and so they were soon withdrawn from the streets. Yet another type was the 'Court' Hansom, which carried two people and had four wheels, but there were not many of these made. In 1887, however, a Mr. Joseph Parlour produced his version of a Hansom which, though two-wheeled, held four people sitting sideways and opposite each other. Entrance was from the rear and through sliding doors which, like that of the 'Tribus', could be operated by the driver from his seat just above them.

Although no new cab designs were successful, many improvements were made on Hansoms and in 1875 Forders, the coachbuilders, won a 1st prize at the Cab and Cab-Horse Show at Alexandra Palace with one supplied to the Prince of Wales—Hansoms having by this time become rather fashionable vehicles. Another instigator of improvements in Hansoms was the Earl of Shrewsbury and Talbot who, in 1880, introduced a new line of Forder-built cabs with rubber-tyred wheels which were less noisy on the streets. In order to attract custom, he revived the practice initiated on the early gentlemen's cabriolets of hanging a little bell on the horses' collars, and this was subsequently copied by many other cab proprietors. Lord Shrewsbury's Hansoms were always clean and meticulously turned out, with his initials "*S. T.*" surmounted by a coronet painted above the windows on either side. On account of his attention to detail he earned the gratitude of the public and considerable animosity from other cab proprietors, who were forced to raise their standards.

By an Act of Parliament in 1838, all drivers of vehicles for hire were forced to take out a licence and to wear a badge which, to the surprise of everyone, was displayed with great pride. This, however, did not ensure either the inspection of working conditions or welfare of the horses and apart from those employed by Lord Shrewsbury, cab horses were, as a rule, pathetically thin and overworked creatures. Unlike those used for buses and trams, whose hours were at least regular, cab horses either had to stand for long periods on cab ranks—often in driving rain and other bad weather conditions—or else be trotted at as high a speed as possible for unbelievably lengthy distances. It was a sad fact that as with coach-horses and those used in post-chaises, the most expensive form of travel was often the worst for the animals involved.

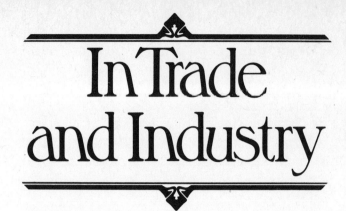

In Trade and Industry

APART FROM THE MANY CAR-riages used for private and public transport, the streets in towns and cities were filled with a large number of commercial vehicles, and there were many tradesmen who took a pride in driving really smart, showy horses and ponies to attract attention and therefore advertise their wares.

The delivery vans belonging to high-class dressmakers and milliners, which were virtually boxed-in Broughams, were turned out as smartly as possible with carriage horses, liveried coachmen and grooms, but some of the smaller tradesmen, such as butchers and fishmongers really stole the scene. The vehicles and turnouts of these two were turned out as smartly as possible with carriage horses, liveried coachmen and grooms, but some of the difference being that fishmongers' vans usually had slatted sides for ventilation. Both drivers wore blue and white aprons—striped horizontally for butchers and vertically

for fishmongers—topped by bowler hats in winter and straw boaters in summer. Of the two, it was perhaps the butchers who were most proud of their horses, insisting upon having smart, fast-trotting ponies—most of them either full or part-bred Hackneys, or else Welsh cobs.

The Brewery Companies also took a great pride in their horses, but on account of the loads involved used heavy breeds such as Shires, Clydesdales, Suffolk Punches and Percherons. Some breweries became famous for the colours and breeds of their horses, as apart from using them for delivery work they also exhibited them at horse shows. In early Georgian days, the vehicle used for the transport of beer in towns was a long two-wheeled dray, which could carry up to five butts of beer, each butt containing 108 gallons. These drays were pulled by two horses harnessed tandem fashion—one in front of the other—and they were urged on by drovers on foot. Later, when smaller casks came to be used, the pair-horse van was

evolved. This was driven from a box-seat and drawn by either a pair of horses or a Unicorn team, and occasionally by a four-in-hand. The Unicorn team became very popular for delivery work, as the single leader could be easily detached from the team and used for lowering or pulling out hogsheads from the cellars of public houses.

Brewers' horses were ponderous and slow moving, but they were immensely compatible to work with, as they learned to stand still for long periods at a time, while the deliveries were being made, and to obey words of com-

Left, below: Brewer's drays and coal carts plying their trades in a snow storm in 1916.
Above: The Vestry horse.
Above, right: It was customary for single-horse coal carts to travel in pairs so that the horses could be used alternatively in tandem as trace-horses to help pull the carts up steep hills.
Below: Distributing milk from a churn in Builth Wells, South Wales.

mand. They developed a high degree of intelligence, for apart from being able to find their own way to their stalls at night, it was said that after a hard day's work, they could, and often did, bring their sleepy and sometimes tipsy drivers safely back to the brewery.

Like the Brewery horses, the cobs used by dairymen developed a great affinity with their drivers and soon learned to walk from house to house and to stand patiently while the milk was delivered. To begin with, they pulled floats containing brass churns, and the milk was ladled out direct into housewives' jugs, but later, when milk was supplied in bottles, special vehicles were constructed to carry crates. These vehicles were fitted with pneumatic tyres and the ponies with composition rubber shoes to lessen the noise which, since milk deliveries always took place at a very early hour in the morning.

Dairy ponies were all strong, cross-bred cobs, many of them with Welsh or Hackney blood in their veins. Most

of them had hogged manes, as this obviated extensive grooming, and their tails were always docked—an operation performed on the majority of harness horses at this time, and done not so much for fashion as for the very real reason that it helped to prevent a horse from getting his tail over the reins.

Like the Brewers, the Dairy companies took great pride in their cobs and many of them were consistent winners in the show ring. Dairy ponies remained great favourites with the public and were one of the last sections of the horse world to be replaced by mechanisation; the reason being that since they walked on their own from house to house at a word of command only, it was difficult to produce a motorised vehicle which could be moved as easily and with so little effort.

Another fine section of the working horse world, but one which rarely received sufficient admiration from the public, were the horses used by undertakers. These were all imported from Holland and of the Friesian breed, a fine, upstanding animal of about 16-hands and with a lot of action. Stallions only were used as it was found that neither mares not geldings retained quite the same gleaming jet-black quality of coat. The harness was black and encrusted with silver fittings, but covered to some extent by long, black velvet loin cloths over the horses' quarters, reaching almost to the ground on either side. Matching ostrich feather plumes nodded on the horses' heads making them an impressive sight. When driven in pairs or as four-in-hands they drew the hearses and mourning carriages proudly, and with dignity.

The horses used by the Fire Brigade and Ambulance services were always stabled in pairs, with their harness hanging above them so that it could be dropped down and fitted with the least possible delay. It was specially constructed for this purpose—the traces fixed directly on to the swingle-trees, which could be hooked up in one movement, instead of having to fit each trace individually. Like the bus horses, they carried a minimum of harness—no pads, belly bands, trace carriers or breechings—but there was an extra strap running from the collar to the traces on which a row of bells was fitted, which provided an extra warning to fellow road-users to get out of the way. These horses were of the strong, vanner type, cross-bred from a cart-horse and a finer type of animal, and the London Fire Brigade in particular insisted upon using only greys. On account of the urgency of their work these horses were allowed to gallop to their destinations.

Horses had, of course, been largely instrumental in helping to build the railways, by transporting workmen,

Previous Two Pages: Tradesmen's carts in London about 1885. The Farringdon Road, with Holborn Viaduct in the background.
Left, top: A London Fire-Brigade dual-purpose appliance drawn by grey horses with bells on their harness.
Left, centre: The funeral of a fireman drawn by black Friesians.
Left, centre (lower): A Metropolitan Police 'Black Maria'—named after an American negress called Maria Lee, from Boston, Mass., who frequently dealt with trouble-makers.
Left: A baker's horse and cart in Wimbledon about 1890.

sleepers and lines, as well as used for excavating and pulling out the earth in tunnels and cuttings. Although the Iron Horse as it was called succeeded eventually in replacing the live variety, the railway companies remained one of the biggest employers of horse power for a very long time.

Apart from the carrying and delivering of all types of freight, both live and inanimate, horses were used on the railway lines to shunt railway carriages and trucks. This was a highly skilled operation, since the horse had to work to a word of command and learn to take a grip on the sleepers with his hind feet, in order to start off the immense weight of the wagons. For this work, a cart-horse, wearing heavy draught harness with chain traces was used. For most other work on the railways, like those used by some of the well-known firms of carriers, a type of heavy vanner was employed, and these were usually worked in pairs.

Another horse whose work was not unlike that of the Shunter's was the Barge horse. These were usually small cart-horses and the barges were attached to them by means of long ropes joined from the masts on the bows of the boats to the swingle trees at the ends of their traces. Barge horses were led along the tow paths of rivers and canals, pulling barges containing loads of as much as 50 tons, until either a lock or a low tunnel forced them to be unhitched. During these encounters with low tunnels, the Barge horse walked over the top while the crew of the barge propelled the boat by lying on their backs and walking the tunnel ceiling, and this was known as "legging" it. Apart from the initial pull to start the load, at which these horses became very expert, the barges usually flowed along fairly easily, but like the Shunter's horse, Barge horses became immensely skilled at taking the weight at crucial and unexpected moments, and when motorised tractors were first used to replace horses, several of them were pulled into the water by the back-lash of these boats!

The work of horses used at seaside resorts for pulling bathing machines was most probably both hard and boring, as they were continually put into the shafts of these machines, which were wooden huts on wheels with doors at the back and steps leading out of them. These they pulled over heavy sand or shingle into the sea, until the water was deemed deep enough for the lady bather inside to make her discreet exit from the machine. Once this was executed, the horse was unhitched to move yet another bather in a machine, and so on, throughout the day. Although limited to the summer months, this work

Right, top: A bathing machine at Yarmouth. The salt water was said to be good for the horse's legs, although the work could be very repetitive.
Right, centre: A carrier's cart in London drawn by a typical Hackney-type cob.
Right: Two Pit Ponies. Horses were used in mines as early as the 17th Century, but on account of their working conditions an Act was passed in 1911 which laid down their hours of work, living conditions, and veterinary inspections.

involved hard pulling and the fact that they were hitched and unhitched so often probably also involved rather rough handling, but the constant immersion in seawater was extremely good for their legs and many working horses were sent to the seaside when their legs would not stand up to any other sort of work.

One section of the working horse community which always received public sympathy, yet was one of the best regulated and organised, was that of ponies working in the coal mines. Pit ponies were used as early as the 17th Century, but on account of criticism of their working conditions an Act was passed in 1911 which laid down their hours, living conditions and veterinary inspections. The ponies varied from the 10 to 12-hand Shetlands for the small seamed mines to 14-hand Dales, Fells and Welsh cobs, and their work consisted of pulling coal tubs along tracks, back and forth, to be emptied and filled. For this work they were fitted with specially designed metal guards to protect their eyes from possible injury, and it was never true that being in the mines sent them blind. Their stables were underground, as it was found that they did better living and working in the same temperature, but there was always a ventilating shaft nearby to provide them with fresh air. At the end of each day the ponies were groomed—in later years with the aid of an electric vacuum cleaner—and as an added precaution against coal dust causing irritation to their skins, their manes were hogged, their heels trimmed and their tails shaved. Not unnaturally, the miners working with ponies became extremely fond of them, and there is no doubt that of all working horses, pit ponies probably suffered the least hardship.

A horse-drawn pleasure boat on the Llangollen Canal.

In the streets of any town, the variety of horses and ponies and the vehicles which they pulled was endless. Every trade was represented and there were also a number of municipal turnouts: The Vestry horse, for instance, was one. This was a heavy cart-horse capable of pulling loads of up to three tons, and used for emptying dustbins and collecting all types of refuse. For this work it was essential to have a horse which would back readily, often up on the pavements. Many of them became very skilled at picking their way over pavements without stepping onto the dangerously fragile glass cellar lights. Their work was hard, about eleven hours a day, during which they would collect and bring in two or three loads. As was the case with the majority of working horses, an affinity developed between them and the men controlling them, and since Vestry horses were rarely driven, but nearly always led, it was said that even the walking gaits of man and beast became identical.

Other hard working horses on the streets were those used by Coal Merchants. These again were cart-horses capable of pulling weights of about three tons, and although their hours were long and the work hard, they did have compensating rests while the coal was delivered. Single horses only were used in Coal Carts, although it was often customary to send out two vehicles together, so that when a particularly steep hill was encountered, one horse could be taken out and attached in front of the other, tandem-wise, to help pull the load to the top. Once there, both horses would be unhitched and led down the hill to the remaining cart, when the procedure would be repeated. On account of this hill-work, the animal charity known as "*Our Dumb Friends' League*" often provided trace horses which, like the cock-horses in coaching days, could be borrowed to help pull heavy loads up steep inclines. "*Our Dumb Friends' League*" was also instrumental in providing water troughs, and although many working horses must have been grateful for them, because of the risk of possible infection, the majority of drivers employed by firms were warned never to let their animals drink from them.

Many horses were used by Government departments, the Post Office being one employer. Apart from the teams used in the early days of mail coaching, which were produced by coach proprietors, there were small, open carts drawn by single horses in which the Guards carried the mail-bags when going to meet the coaches at the various starting or stopping places. In the country, the mails were often delivered in small, closed carts, not unlike those used by butchers, and drawn by a single horse. There were also large vans for transporting parcels, to which four-in-hands of fast trotters were driven.

All the vehicles used by the Post Office were painted scarlet and had the words "*Royal Mail*", together with the Royal cypher, painted on either side, which made them sufficiently conspicuous for the Police, and also for other road users to give them free passage when possible. Another vehicle to be known by its colour was the dreaded pair-horse closed van with barred windows, known

'Hercules', the coster horse, at work in London.

as the Black Maria, which was used by the Police to transport prisoners and criminals, and this, like the Royal Mail, the Fire Brigade and Ambulance services, received priority in traffic.

In addition to all these different vehicles, there were large numbers of carrier's carts which were used for the transport of anything which required shifting. Furniture vans and Pantechnicons, drawn by Unicorn teams, were often to be seen, and since there were no refrigerators, blocks of ice could be purchased from Ice Carts, a business usually run by Italians, but in the summer only. Special carts were built for carrying cattle, sheep and pigs and there were animal ambulances and Knacker's vans for transporting sick as well as dead animals—many of them casualties in the streets, for it was not unusual to find horses injured or killed by having been trodden on, knocked down, and even run over by passing turnouts. Horseboxes were rarely seen in London, as most horses which could not be driven were either led by men on foot or tied on behind another vehicle and made to trot, although it was sometimes necessary in the country, and particularly where race-horses were involved, for them to be transported from place to place by horsebox.

In towns, it was customary for firms employing large numbers of horses, and particularly those who required them for specialised jobs, to have their own stables, but there were many smaller tradesmen and other people who could not afford the upkeep which this involved. It was for these people that the service provided by Jobmasters fulfilled a need.

The stables of Jobmasters contained a large variety of horses—from smart, upstanding carriage horses, fast trotting cobs, strong vanners, to those used for heavy drays. Any animal, in fact, which might be needed, and all, if the Jobmaster was to be successful, of as high a standard as possible. Jobmasters supplied horses to many professional men, such as doctors, for it was essential for them to have a horse ready to go out at a moment's notice, and if it was ill, or went lame, then to be able to call for a replacement. Similarly, it was useful for organisations such as the Police and Fire Brigades to have horses provided, and the firm of Thomas Tilling, one of the biggest Jobmasters in London, had a stud containing 2,300 horses of all sorts, sizes and colours—greys being required for weddings as well as for use by the Fire Brigade.

Another section of the horse-drawn world, and one which is still active today, is the Costermonger. Everything about them is traditional, from their gaily decorated and painted four-wheeled trolleys to their harness with its flashes of brightly coloured leather beneath the metal fittings. Costers are, and always have been, excellent judges of horse-flesh, using high-stepping, fast-trotting ponies and cobs, many of them from Wales, and on festive occasions they are decorated by having their manes and tails neatly plaited and tied up with pom-poms made of brightly coloured wool and ribbons.

The work of the costermonger, which involves the collection of all types of scrap from both houses and shops, entails for the ponies long hours of walking, stopping and standing unattended on the streets, and they have always been among the best trained for this purpose. On account of the nature of their work, the loads vary in weight from day to day, but most of the ponies are well cared for and fed and can be seen trotting freely home to their stables at night. With the increasing difficulties of both finding and remaining in suitable back yards, and the rising costs of fodder and shoeing, it is more than likely that costermongers may have to give up their ponies in favour of mechanised transport, but it will be a sad day for England when this is so.

On the Land

THE HISTORY OF THE HORSE IN agriculture is not a long one, as nearly all countries considered the slow-moving but powerful ox to be far superior for all forms of heavy transport. It was not, therefore, until the introduction of the heavy breeds of cart-horses into Northern Europe, as well as North America, in the late 17th Century that horses began to supersede oxen, and even to in much of Southern Europe, the whole of Africa and Asia ox teams were still preferred. In most Latin countries and in the southern states of North America the horse's illegitimate cousin the mule was considered more suitable than either horses or oxen, and in dry countries the mule's hardiness and toughness made it an ideal animal for draught.

In England there are three breeds of heavy cart-horses— the Shire, the Clydesdale and the Suffolk Punch—and farmers soon found it profitable to work teams of these horses in all agricultural gears. Usually, the mares were kept for work on the farm and for breeding, and the geldings sold to the cities to satisfy the ever-growing demand for heavy draught horses. The Shires, said to be the lineal descendants of the old English war horse, are perhaps the heaviest and most powerful of all, and were bred mostly in the Midlands—the Welsh Shire being slightly smaller.

Shires are bred in every colour except chestnut. Clydesdales, as their name implies, originate from the lowlands of Scotland and the border breeders supplied them to the industrial Midlands, and also to Canada and the USA where they were much in demand. The Clydesdale is slightly longer in the leg than the Shire and has far more white about him—on his face and up his legs almost up to his belly at times. They are also bred in most colours, with the addition of roan. Suffolk horses, or Punches as they are sometimes called, are one of the oldest breeds, dating back to 1506. They are always chestnut in colour, of seven recognised shades, and whereas the other two breeds have feather on their legs, the Suffolks are clean limbed—making them ideally suited to the heavy arable lands of their native Eastern counties.

At one time, every type of farm vehicle and wagon was horse-drawn, and the construction of implements varied according to the area in which they were used. In Scotland, hay was carted on low two-wheeled, single horse 'bogies', while in the south of England massive wagons drawn by two or more horses were used—each county having its own special design of wagon. In British farming, it was not usual to employ big teams and the three horse binder was normally the largest hitch—three horses abreast being employed—but in the wheat belts of the United States, Canada and Australia it was normal to use fantastically large implements and big teams.

The well-known forty-horse hitch, much publicised by the showmen *Barnum and Bailey*, was really a circus turn, but hitches of twenty-four horses or mules to the big combine harvesters were not unusual. In farming, the number of horses required obviously depended on the acreage and on the type of farming carried out, and a very rough guide was one horse to every thirty acres on a mixed farm, and a plough team of three horses and one plough-man would be expected to work sixty acres of arable land, though again this might vary according to the type of land. An acre could be ploughed by one pair in six to eight hours, provided that the field was a regular size, and ideally the furrows would be 220 yards long—in fact a furlong (furrow long).

The use of horses on the land was twofold: to work and to breed, and in many areas, particularly grassland farming areas, horses which were not strictly *cart*-horses were used. The Fell ponies of Westmorland and Cumberland and the Dale ponies of Yorkshire were examples of ponies well able to carry out all the draught requirements of a small farm, and at the same time be useful as riding ponies for shepherds or farmers, as well as being driven into market when required. The Welsh Cob was another small but versatile animal which was useful on a farm as well as being in great demand in the towns as a tradesman's delivery cob.

In Ireland, where most farms were small and predominently grass, the famous Irish draught horse was developed. This was a clean-legged animal of about 16-hands, with plenty of bone and substance, and well able to do any job on a farm. At the same time, they made very adequate riding horses, and having jumped Irish banks and ditches from birth they could hold their own when out hunting. Mares of this breed, crossed with a thorough-bred stallion, produced excellent heavy-weight hunters and first-class steeplechase horses. Many top show jumpers have originated from Irish draught mares. It is a great pity

that due to mechanisation this fine breed of horse is in danger of extinction.

Apart from work on farms, horses were also extensively used in the forests, and these were probably the most intelligent and well trained of all working horses since they had to pull logs, often out of heavy mud, and load them onto wagons, controlled only by the forester's word of command. Although used singly for light loads, a tandem, or even a team of four were employed when the occasion demanded it. Weight pulling competitions were often held, and in Britain were frequently won by pairs of Clydesdales, which were the property of the Liverpool Dock Authority. However, the largest load ever pulled on land must have been the timber load of approximately 125 tons, hauled on a sledge by a pair of Shires over a quarter of a mile of icy road in Michigan, USA, in 1893.

Cart-horse harnesses were often very ornate and, as if the hard working carters did not have enough to do, a great deal of time was required to polish and embellish it. Superstition played a large part in their lives, and numerous designs of horse brasses were attached to the harness —to bring good luck or to ward off the evil eye. These are believed to have been in use as long ago as in Roman times and were first worn on the face-piece—which hangs from the brow band, between the horse's eyes. By tradition, this brass represented the sun, but occasionally there were two and sometimes three different designs.

Above: Day-break on an Essex farm.
Left: Ploughing in bad weather.
Right, above: Harvesting with a binder.
Right: Haymaking on a hay 'Bogie'.

Further down the head, the nose-band held a brass which was hinged, so as to curve over the horse's nose, and here the maker of the harness would sometimes inscribe his name and address. Further down still, and hanging between the horse's fore-legs, was the martingale, which was attached from the hames of the collar to the belly-band, and could carry as many as nine or ten brasses. A large number of these martingales were sold complete with brasses, but there were carters who liked making up their own—some choosing to have a set of identical brasses, while others preferred a varied selection. These brasses were made in many different designs, although there were one or two standard patterns adopted by big companies: Millers and Corn merchants, for instance,

might use brasses containing a wheatsheaf, while the Brewers would have either a barrel, or else their firm's trademark, which, in its turn, stemmed from the family's heraldic crest.

Apart from these standard pieces of harness decorated by brasses, there were a number of extra straps, such as rein hangers, side, rib, hip or loin straps, which were placed across the horses' backs and could be similarly adorned. Other items, such as trace carriers, saddles, bridles and winkers were also heavily encrusted with brass, either by buckles, or else by monograms, crests or trademarks. Other features of cart-horse harnesses were fly terrets and latten bells. Fly terrets, known locally in different parts of the country as swingers, danglers, nod-

Haymaking in the Lake District.

Harrowing with Clydesdale Horses in South-West Scotland.

ders, top-knots, top-notchers and leaders, are situated on top of the bridle, between and behind the ears, and usually consist of a miniature brass swinging within a ring, which in turn was topped by a plume made of horse-hair, dyed red, white, and blue. Apart from their decorative value, these were useful in that with the constant movement of a horse's head, flies were kept at bay. Only the leaders of a team were allowed to wear them, however, as it was essential that they should be able to hear words of command, but the horse behind them, for whom this was not so necessary, were provided with ear-caps.

Latten bells, apart from being yet another decoration, were used for warning oncoming traffic, and consisted of rows of bells made of brass which could be fitted into the horses' saddles or pads. These bells, made in different sizes, emitted the varying tones of bass, tenor, alto and treble, and it was customary to fit the largest and therefore the deepest sounding bells to the leaders. It was also usual for the bells to be made in sets of three, four, five and six—the highest toning ones consisting of the greater number. As can be imagined, many horses had to be acclimatised to the sound of these bells which, together with the jingle of pole and trace chains, as well as other pieces of equipment, formed a noisy, if musical, accompaniment to their movements.

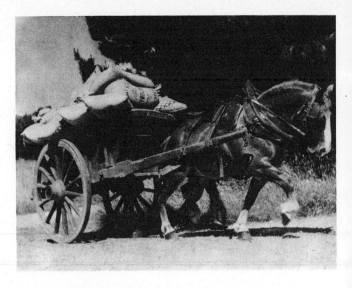

Above: Pulling a heavy load in a tip-cart in France.
Below: A combine harvester pulled by more than thirty horses in an Oregon wheat field about 1880.
Right: Carting potatoes, one of the many tasks of the heavy draught horse in farming.
Right, below: This load, consisting of fifty pine logs, collectively weighing over 125 tons, was pulled on a sledge along a level ice road for a quarter of a mile by a pair of English shire horses in Michigan, USA, in 1893.

In the mid-19th Century, hundreds of horses were used in connection with the construction of the railways which, inevitably, were destined to contribute to the near extinction of the heavy horse. In railway building, one problem was the tunnelling-out and building-up of the massive earthworks constituting the embankments. Clearly, it was impossible for horses to pull loads of earth up the steep faces of an embankment, so an ingenious method was employed whereby a sledge full of earth at the bottom was attached to a rope which passed over a pulley at the top. A horse was harnessed to the rope and encouraged to trot down the steep bank. When the sledge reached the required height, the earth was released by a trip mechanism and the horse was then led to the top, and the process repeated.

Besides the different jobs on the land in the usual agricultural implements, horses provided the power for a variety of static appliances such as water pumps, stationary threshers, root cutters and hay lifts. All these required the services of either a horse, a pony, or even a donkey, to perform the boring and laborious task of walking endlessly in a circle, but today there is really no place for horses on the land. Even the few jobs such as working in the confined rows of fruit or hop gardens—at one time the prerogative of the horse—have now been mechanised, and for all heavy work the tractor has long since superseded the horse. Fortunately, there are still a number of enthusiasts in Great Britain who enjoy working with horses and this has saved the heavy horse breeds from complete extinction. Indeed, by means of classes for heavy horses at Agricultural shows there remains a demand both in England, as well as overseas, for heavy horses.

In addition to the three English breeds of cart-horse, a number from the Continent were imported. These consisted of chestnut horses from Belgium, who were slightly smaller than Suffolk Punches and popular for use as strong Vanners, and Percherons from France. Percherons were always grey and clean limbed, which many farmers liked, and some drove them in the French style; with only one rein attached to the left side of their mouths and they responded to slight pulls or jerks accompanied by words of command. Both these breeds were used with success for cross-breeding, and Percherons in particular have remained in Britain ever since.

THERE IS PROBABLY NO FIELD IN which the horse has given man more faithful and devoted service than in war. Apart from the vast numbers of horses used throughout the ages for cavalry, or other mounted troops, even more have been required for draught, and it is these, rather than the chargers, who can be said to have produced the horse power.

The first use of horse power in war was undoubtedly the war chariot, originated probably by the Assyrians. Chariots were in turn adopted by the Persian, Egyptian,

Greek and Roman civilisations. Their use in war was twofold: first, to strike terror into the enemy, and secondly to convey archers and javelin throwers quickly into battle. The later chariots were constructed to carry a crew of as many as six warriors—two of whom would hold shields, two would drive and two would shoot the arrows. The war chariot led the way for wheeled transport for supplies, and Sennacherib in his campaign against Babylon (705 to 680 BC) is recorded to have taken 7,200 horses and mules, as well as 11,073 asses—which gives some idea of the size of the transport involved.

At about the same time that the war chariot was developed in the Middle East, chariots and wagons had been introduced into China, and in the *Chou* period (1027 to 223 BC), standards of weights were prescribed for wheeled vehicles, fast driving was prohibited, and roads classified for different types of traffic. There is every reason to suppose that the Chinese were ahead of the Western World, and were the first to use collars and shafts, as opposed to yokes and poles, thus improving the draught as well as increasing the speed of the vehicles. The Chinese charioteers went to war with a great deal of ceremony and to a very strict ritual. The chariots were hung with clattering ornaments and bells and the harness was most ornate. Four horses abreast were normally used, although the outside horses could have little effect on the speed of the vehicle. The charioteer, holding six reins, stood in the centre, with an archer on his left and a lance-man on his right. All three were protected by armour made of three layers of ox-hide. War chariots were used extensively by the Greeks and Romans, and almost the last users of chariots for war were the Celts in Britain.

Gradually, the chariot ceased to be used as an implement of war, and it was replaced by mounted cavalry. Draught horses were not an important factor in war until the introduction of mobile artillery, ammunition and food supply wagon trains, several centuries later.

The pulling of guns by horses preceded the organised use of military supply transport by many years. Throughout the ages, gun horses have always been postillion ridden—as opposed to being driven in long reins. Artillery horses varied from the cart-horses used for the heavy Field Batteries to the small but strong riding horses which were capable of pulling the light horse artillery guns into action at the gallop. A great deal of thought was also always given to types of harness and equipment used for the teams—composed usually of six horses, which pulled the guns. Breast collars and leather covered chain-and-wire traces were used—both fitted with quick-release attachments so that the horses could be taken out in a matter of seconds, in case of accidents.

It was not until the middle of the 19th Century that organised military transport was used, for carting rations, supplies and ammunition. Prior to this, armies had lived off the country, by pressing local transport into service. Apart from first line transport, which was attached to units in the field, the bulk of supplies were the responsibility of the *Royal Army Service Corps* (now the *Royal Corps of Transport*).

There were a variety of different carts and wagons devised for special military purposes, although the standard types of vehicle used by the British Army were the Maltese cart, the AT (Animal Transport) cart, and the GS (General Service) wagon. Other countries adopted slightly different military transport, according to their requirements and conditions. The French, in particular, used a heavier vehicle drawn by three horses abreast, called the *"Chariot du Parc"*. The Maltese cart was a light, two-

Top: Chariot racing in ancient Rome.
Centre: A pair of heavy-draught horses in the First World War.
Above: A column of ammunition limbers.
Opposite page, top: A gun carriage.
Opposite page, centre: Horses being fitted with gas masks.
Opposite page, bottom: Horses pulling an ambulance.

wheeled single horse cart mostly used as first line transport, while the AT cart, used primarily in India, was a two-wheeled cart with a pole, drawn by two horses or mules, and the system of draught could be either 'pole and neck bar', 'pole and belly bugle', or 'Tonga curricle draught'.

In the first of these systems the pole is supported on a bar which hangs in front of the horses' chests, and was used extensively in South Africa. In the second system, the pole is fixed to a belly bugle, which consists of two semi-circular pieces of metal which pass under the animal's body and are attached by straps to the pad, or saddle. In Tonga, or curricle draught, the end of the pole is attached to a cross-piece of metal or wood fixed to the animal's saddle, and was in current use in India.

The GS wagon was a strongly built four-wheeled wagon drawn by a team of two or four horses, or mules, which could either be driven from the box seat or ridden postillion.

These wagons were the standard supply vehicles up to the First World War, and with a team of four horses or mules were capable of pulling 3,000 lbs of almost any type of load over difficult country. Ambulances, Field kitchens, Engineers and Signallers wagons of all sorts were horse-drawn, and in some areas of warfare, horses and mules were used extensively for pack transport, carrying loads of supplies and ammunition, the load being 160 lbs an animal.

During the First World War the numbers of transport horses involved was astronomical, and the casualties very heavy. In 1918, when quite a lot of transport had been mechanised, there were still 428 Army Service Corps animal transport companies in the various theatres of war, which would have involved over 70,000 horses or mules, and this only included transport from base or rail-head. Each fighting unit would have its own establishment of

transport animals, and although heavy artillery was mechanised, vast numbers of horses were required for field and light guns.

It is difficult to imagine how the Remount department set about satisfying this vast demand for horses. All private and most trade horses were commandeered at the outbreak of war and horses and mules were shipped in large numbers from other countries, principally the Argentine and Canada.

No one who has witnessed the casualties and suffering undergone by horses in times of war can be sorry that they have now been replaced by mechanical transport, and their present military role is purely ceremonial.

In North America

THERE IS NOT MUCH DOUBT THAT the first horses to reach the North American continent were imported by the Spanish explorers through Mexico, and were of Arab origin. Horses certainly took to the American climate and conditions and multiplied enormously. In return, the Red Indian inhabitants of both the South and West reciprocated by speedily becoming good horse masters and riders of great skill.

Curiously, the Indians, although they occasionally used a type of sledge with shafts, the ends of which dragged along the ground, never adopted the wheel or used any form of vehicle as a means of transport. Had they done so, it is possible that the whole development of the Western States might have taken a very different course.

The Pilgrim Fathers imported horse-drawn vehicles to the East Coast, but these were mainly utility carts such as wagons. Later, the early colonists imported European carriages of every type. At the same time, various designs of purely American vehicles were being developed. It was soon found that the light and elegant carriages of English design were not suitable for the very rough roads or long distances involved. Furthermore, European town vehicles had been designed to suit old cities with narrow streets and tight turns.

American vehicles therefore were constructed very strongly with large wheels, long wheel bases and often very restricted turning locks. During the War of American Independence, it was forbidden by Congress to import English carriages. This encouraged not only the increase in American designs, but also the production of European designed vehicles in America. Those with four wheels were favoured, of which the most popular was the well-known buggy. Light, but strong, and seating two persons, it was pulled by either a single horse or a pair. Rockaways, of which there were several designs,

were basically four-wheeled, pair-horse vehicles with a high roof, the sides either glazed or open, protected only by a curtain. This design was later to be copied by the manufacturers of limousine motor cars.

A similar vehicle was the Surrey, often with a fringe on top, and much favoured in the South. The Buckboard, made from a single board supported on four wheels, and named on account of its tendency to behave like a Bronco on the unmade roads of the West, was also a light but very strong four-wheeled utility pair-horse carriage. One of the few American two-wheeled vehicles was the Meadowbrook cart, a type of skeleton gig for two persons. Various kinds of two- and four-wheeled sulkies were developed, and a type of rustic phaeton known as a Bronson wagon.

In the later part of the 19th Century and early 20th

Century, driving became very popular, particularly on the Eastern Seaboard. Millionaires would vie with each other on the smartness of their turnouts at Newport, Rhode Island and other fashionable centres. All types of British and continental carriages and coaches were imported or manufactured in the States, many by the most famous of all American coachbuilders, J. Brewster.

From the early breed of horses introduced into the country from Spain there developed a wiry, hard, lithe horse equally useful as a ranch horse or between the shafts, which was particularly popular since speed was more necessary than extravagant action. From this horse the type later to be known as a Quarter horse was developed. Two other American breeds also played important parts as harness horses, the Morgan and the Standard Bred.

The breed of Morgan horses was originated in the late 18th Century by a singing master from Vermont, named Justin Morgan, who was given a little bay stallion in payment for a debt. Named after him, this horse became

famous by winning a number of weight-pulling competitions, and as a sire he stamped himself so effectively on his progeny that they too made their names. Morgan horses are sturdy little animals of about 15-hands, with beautiful heads and superb action, and are equally suitable for riding or harness work. One of Justin Morgan's most celebrated descendents was the great trotting stallion Ethan Allen, who took part in many trotting matches, the most famous in 1867 against a well-known racing trotter named Dexter. Ethan Allen ran with a thoroughbred "*running mate*"—this practice was not unusual, the theory being, that the "*running mate*", who was attached to the sulky as a pair but with shorter traces, galloped and took all the weight of the vehicle, leaving the other horse to trot free. Ethan Allen and mate beat Dexter in three heats of a mile each, timed at 2·15, 2·16 and 2·19 minutes.

The Standard Bred is exclusively a harness breed of horse and through the famous stallion Messenger has its origin in the same lines from which the British Thorough-

Left: An American Baker's van.
Top: Lumber being moved on a sledge. This was the usual way to move timber during the winter in Northern areas.
Above: Harvesting maize with a four-horse team. The leading pair of horses are urged on by a drover on foot at their side.

bred stock was founded. They are small, wiry horses bred for speed as trotters or pacers, and used for harness racing, which is immensely popular in the United States and Canada. Both trotters and pacers of this breed have done a mile in under two minutes. The trotting record, held by Nevele Pride, is a mile in 1 minute 54·8 seconds and for pacing is held by Bret Hanover in 1 minute 54 seconds.

The wagon used in Colonial America to carry freight was an enormously heavy vehicle known as the Conestoga wagon, which originated in Lancaster County, Pennsylvania. Shaped more like a boat than a wagon, it had a barrel-shaped top made of canvas and was pulled by six heavy horses, the near-wheeler ridden by the wagoner who controlled the other five horses by means of a single rein and by his voice. From this wagon the slightly smaller prairie schooner was developed which was used by the early pioneers of the West and normally pulled by teams of oxen or mules, rather than by horses.

The most famous of all American vehicles was the Con-cord Coach, much glamorised by Western films. Very similar to the mud wagons from which it was developed, the Concord Coach was built by Abbot Downing at Concord, New Hampshire, as an overland stage coach. It weighed over a ton and stood 8 feet high and 5½ feet wide. Very sturdily built, the body was slung on thorough brace springs made of layers of ox-hide, which helped both coach and team over rough roads and cushioned the occupants from the worst joltings. The inside was designed to hold nine passengers—three in each of the two high-backed seats and three more on a 'jump' seat set up between the doors of the coach, which had a movable leather back rest. When full, it certainly must have been very constricted. The outside accommodated a further seven passengers, plus the driver and messenger, whose duties corresponded to those of the Guard on English Mail coaches. A large boot under the box seat and a rear boot supported by chains and covered by a leather apron provided space for mail and luggage.

Four or six horses or mules were used to pull these coaches and were changed every ten to twenty miles. Well fed and cared for, the horses did their stages year after year. It is recorded that one horse in California did his stage every day for fifteen years—nearly a quarter of a million miles. When six horses were driven, the middle pair had a loose pole slung between them and were known as the *swings*. The drivers, who were extremely skilled, did not adopt the English method of holding all the reins in the left hand but drove two-handed, holding the near two or three reins in the left hand and the off reins in the right.

There were many overland routes in the West in the 1860s. One of the most famous routes was the Central overland route of 1,913 miles from Atchison, Kansas, to Placerville, California. The journey was accomplished in nineteen days and the passenger fare was $325. The trip was made up of three divisions: the Eastern—Atchison to Denver; the Mountain—Denver to Salt Lake City; and the Western—Salt Lake City to Placerville. Each division was cut up into 200 mile sections and each section into stages, with stations every ten to fifteen miles.

For many years Benjamin Holladay's Overland Stage Company controlled this route but in 1866 sold to the famous Wells Fargo Company. A few years later, however, the transcontinental railway was completed and by 1870 Concord Coaches were replaced by steam over the trans-continental routes.

One of the most typical of North American Western vehicles was the Chuckwagon, immortalised by the

Previous Two Pages: A 'stopping place' on the road in 1868 where the horses were fed, watered and rested. The buggies, light but strongly constructed, were pulled by either a single horse or a pair and seated two persons.
Right: A team of four in a farm wagon.
Below: A team of express furniture and piano removers using a pair-horse van.
Centre, below: A water-cart in operation, with shade for the driver.
Right, below: A Merchant's van.

65

Left: A horse-drawn hearse.
Above: A small estate fire appliance.
Below: A street scene with a Hansom cab. A pair-horse omnibus rolls forward with umbrellas held high over the passengers to repell the untimely rain.
Right: The grace and style of the Hansom Cab is outlined against the columns of a stately home. The driver, sitting at the rear, had the difficult task of guiding the horse in and out of city traffic—and he could see only the horse's ears.

Chuckwagon races first staged at the Calgary Sampede in 1923 by showman Guy Weadlock. Chuckwagon races provide the highlight and offer the highest prize money at Calgary. They have also been adopted as a top spectacle by some of the larger Rodeos in the United States, principally at Cheyenne Rodeo, Wyoming.

Left: The exitement and drama of the ChuckWagon race at the world-famous Calgary Stampede, first staged by showman Guy Weadlock.
Above: Trotting ponies in full flight around a track in Wisconsin. Trotting races are very popular, and often held as part of festivals and fairs, especially when fruits are harvested.
Below: A well-known Standard-bred horse, Lady De Jarnette, exhibited by her owner Mr. W. H. Wilson.

On the signal to start, the wagons have to be loaded with kitchen stoves and other stores by mounted escorts and they then race, first over a twisting course between barrels and then round the arena, as though the Indians were after them. The escorts have to mount their excited horses and be level with the wagon at the finishing line. Needless to say, the driving of these wagons is highly skilled and very dangerous, providing as it does a most exciting spectacle.

There are some small pockets in the United States where the driving of horses is still very much alive. These are principally in the Pennsylvania Dutch areas of Southern Pennsylvania. Here, and in many other isolated spots in the Northern States, the Menonites and their offshoot, the Amish people, are barred by their religious beliefs from using mechanical aids to farming and so use horses for all forms of transport. In some villages on the Sabbath, dozens of typical Amish square boxed-in carriages can be seen parked outside the meeting house.

As in other parts of the world, there has been a great revival of driving in the United States in recent years. Despite the very large distances involved, driving classes are well supported in shows in the States and in Canada. In particular, the Devon Show in Pennsylvania always has well-filled classes for the driving of singles and pairs as well as for coaches, and driving enthusiasts are well catered for at the Royal Winter Fair held in Toronto in November.

The Carriage Association of America has a strong membership and arranges meetings and rallies throughout the States as well as producing a most informative publication, *"The Carriage Journal"*, which is brought out quarterly.

In Ireland

BECAUSE THERE WAS NO REALLY heavy transport on them, the roads in Ireland in the 18th Century were in a better state than those in England, and although English coaches had been imported, the majority of people could not afford to patronise them. A system of Post-horses did exist, but this again was for the wealthy, as each stage, which consisted of about fifteen to twenty miles, cost £2 and there were also the additional and not inconsiderable charges for turnpikes.

Most travellers, therefore, either walked or rode on horseback, or, in some cases, combined the two by adopting the method known as "*Walk and Ride*". In this way two people could, with one horse between them, cover quite long distances by the following means: both persons set out together, with one walking and the other riding, and after the horseman had covered about five miles, he tied the horse up somewhere along the road, and continued on foot. When the walker reached the horse, he mounted, and passing his companion, secured the horse a few miles further on, and so the procedure was repeated until the end of the journey.

For those with luggage, or who did not wish to ride, various small vehicles could be hired for short distances only, at a cost of about 6d a mile—the one principally used being the ubiquitous Jaunting Car. This vehicle is peculiar to Ireland, and the only one built with two wheels and to be drawn by a single horse, yet with accommodation for five or more persons. Two, or in some cases three, passengers sat back to back on either side facing outwards over the wheels, with the driver, or 'jarvey' as he was sometimes called, on a central and forward-facing seat at the front. There was another variety known as the 'Inside' car, which was not unlike the English Governess cart in appearance but with the driver's seat out and in front. In this vehicle the passengers sat facing inwards—access being reached by a small door at the rear—but

although it had the advantage of being safer, in that the people could not fall out, it lacked the dash and excitement afforded by the 'Outside' car.

In addition to the Jaunting car, some other purely Irish vehicles plied for hire in Dublin during the 18th and early 19th Centuries. One was called the 'Ringsend' car, and was a single horse carriage, the seat of which was suspended on leather braces between the shafts. Another was the 'Noddy', which was said to have been used only by the lower classes. This was a low, covered, single horse vehicle in which the driver sat crouched behind the horse's rump, with the passenger close behind him, and the shafts were so sloping that as it moved along it nodded— which accounted for the name. A third type was the 'Jingle' which, although described as looking like a coach "*after the doors, upper sides, and roof had been removed*", was very popular and used by much more respectable people. This was drawn by a single horse, but held six passengers who were charged 6d a head for travelling a specified and short distance within the town. It is also reported that it made a jingling noise when in transit—which was the reason for its name.

By the beginning of the 19th Century, the Mail Coaches, which were run along much the same lines as those in England, began to be better patronised, with as many as forty operating out of Dublin. Although there were Stage Coaches—some of which held nearly twenty passengers —none of them, in spite of the excellent condition of the roads, ever attained quite the same degree of perfection or popularity as in England. A first-class system of public transport came to Ireland from a most unlikely and surprising source. In 1802, a sixteen-year-old Italian boy called Carlo Bianconi arrived in Ireland to sell small and cheap engravings and religious prints, and within four years he had opened his own shop and was working as a carver and gilder. His experience of travelling about the country selling his wares had brought home to him the inadequacy of the transport system then in existence, so he applied his gift for organisation to the initiation of the first cheap method of conveying the public between the smaller towns and villages.

In 1815, Bianconi put his first vehicle on a scheduled service between the towns of Clonmel and Cahir, a distance of only ten miles. This was a humble 'Side-car' which carried only four passengers and was pulled by one horse, but to begin with the service was not a success. Bianconi countered this, however, by producing another vehicle which was thought to be a rival and soon both

Above: A peat merchant in Connemara, where he takes the same
position in the country villages as the English coalman.
Left: A Jaunting or Side-car driven by the Jarvey. The
passengers sat facing outwards on a well-sprung chassis with
two or in some cases three either side.

cars were filled to capacity every day. The business pros-
pered and by the end of the year he was able to link Clonmel with both Limerick and Thurles. The following year
more lines were opened until by 1825 his cars were covering over 1,000 miles a day.

Bigger vehicles (known as 'Massey Dawsons', after a
local landlord) were built to carry ten passengers, but the
load was found to be too great for one horse, so a second
was attached by means of a swingle-tree, and worked
alongside. These cars soon proved too small to cater for
the growing demand and so even larger vehicles with
four wheels and capable of carrying twenty passengers
were produced. These were called 'Finn McCools', after
a mythical Irish giant, and were similar in design to the
original Jaunting cars in that the passengers still sat on
either side facing outwards, but they were made more
comfortable by upholstered seats. Leather aprons were
provided to protect passengers from cold and wet.

Bianconi was always immensely proud of his horses
and in the early days had been able to obtain a good stamp
of animal by buying those bred for the Army when, due
to the cessation of the Napoleonic Wars, they were no
longer needed. Apart, however, from ensuring that his
horses were well fed and housed, and had Sundays as a

Above: Bianconi cars being unloaded outside an Irish Hotel. Much of the early travel in Ireland resulted from the business acumen and endeavours of Carlo Biancone, an Italian boy who arrived in Ireland in 1802 at the age of sixteen.
Right: An agricultural tip-cart.

day of rest, he liked to see them impeccably turned out. From his original two-wheeled one-horse cars, pairs had been put to his four-wheeled vehicles, with the addition on some trips of a single leader, to make a Unicorn team, while on other journeys a four-in-hand was used. The Bianconi cars were smartly painted, red and yellow being the predominant colours, with the names of the towns picked out in gold letters at the back, for he saw the advertising value of his turnouts. Although he had long since given up the business of art dealing, his eye for pictures was as acute as ever, so when a young artist produced paintings of the Bianconi equipages, he persuaded *Ackerman of London* to engrave and reproduce them in sets, for sale in the towns through which the vehicles passed.

By 1830, Bianconi had opened up routes all over Ireland, and although the big coach proprietors, such as Purcell & Co. of Dublin, ran mail and stage coaches out of the capital, his success lay in the fact that the 'Bians' (as they were called) provided transport *between* the main coaching roads. Bianconi continued to run his cars for many years after the railways had infiltrated the country, but he was astute enough to vary his services to suit the trains, and in 1861, when railways had been in operation for nearly thirty years, he still covered over 4,000 miles

of roads and employed more than 900 horses. From a humble beginning, Bianconi had become a national institution and had provided a most useful service to the country of his adoption. He died in 1875, a wealthy and much respected citizen of Clonmel.

Apart from the vehicles used for public transport in Ireland, there were a number of private carriages of different sizes and shapes owned and used by those who could afford them. Some coaches were imported from England, but the carriage building industry developed in Ireland until by 1849 there were twenty-five such firms in Dublin alone. The Great Exhibition there in 1865 produced, as it did in England, many unusual and fanciful designs, among them a private Jaunting car built by Killinger, which had seats covered in superbly buttoned upholstery edged with matching braid, while the driver's seat was elegantly poised on arched ironwork supports at the *back* of the carriage, instead of the more usual position at the front.

Ireland was, and still is, famous for horse-breeding, and Thoroughbreds in particular. In addition, the well-known Irish Draught Horse, which contains Clydesdale

Above: Taking milk to the creamery in Co. Cork—a leisurely way of life which must be the envy of many people.
Right: A blacksmith's shop at Abbeyfeale, Co. Limerick, where the picturesque appeal of horses always draws a crowd of sight-seers.

blood, was used extensively for all types of heavy and commercial transport, as well as for crossing purposes. On the West Coast, ponies of the Connemara breed were excellent for drawing all types of small vehicles and Jaunting cars, while Cobs, those mysteriously bred, strong, sturdy and clown-like little horses, abounded in the country.

No chronicle of driving in Ireland would be complete without mention of the Gypsies, or Tinkers as they are called. The climate and general conditions suited them ideally and many swarmed the countryside with their caravans pulled by heavy cobs—often accompanied by loose foals. The Barrel-topped van was more favoured by Tinkers than the more embellished wagons, such as the Showman's, Reading, Leeds or Ledge vans found in England. Tinkers are natural horse dealers, and they travelled extensively to transact deals of every sort.

On the Continent

MANY TYPES OF HORSE-drawn carriages were known and used all over the world, although some countries produced their own individual vehicles or developed different and specialised styles of harness and driving, while others became known for their breeds of horses.

On the Continent, Hungary was perhaps the country most associated with driving and carriages, for it is believed that the word 'coach' evolved from the village of Kocs (which although spelled differently in various manuals, is pronounced as *coach*). Kocs was the centre of Hungary's Royal coachbuilders and it is said that heavy four-wheeled vehicles were made there as early as during the 9th Century, for the Magyar tribes.

In Hungary the owning of horses became, as elsewhere, a status symbol, and it was not unusual to see teams of four, five, six or even seven horses being driven about the country. The Hungarian method of driving has always differed from that used in England, together with a considerably lighter type of harness—breast collars being preferred to the full and heavier collars favoured by some countries. This was highly and gaily decorated with bells, ornate brass-work and buckles, with fringes and tassels of every sort, and always individually made. As in England, the liveries worn by coachmen and grooms varied in colour with the different families.

At one time it had been considered essential to drive teams of horses from a high box-seat, but in Hungary they were often driven from small, light and low phaeton-like vehicles, one of which, the Eszterhazy, named after the well-known family, became immensely popular. For these carriages, a light and prancing type of horse was required, and the Arab, the Lipizzaner, or a cross of these two, which were mostly greys, were the breeds most favoured. For those, however, who preferred teams of black or dark brown horses, two other breeds existed. The Nonius was one, and these are bred in two distinct sizes—over and under 15·3-hands, and are therefore denominated as *Large* or *Small*; while the other, the Furiosos, were to become so popular that the Prince Ludwig of Bavaria continues to breed them in Southern Germany.

A German rail-car in Berlin about 1866. This highly decorated double-decker vehicle was known as a Charlottenburg omnibus. The life expectancy of horses pulling rail-cars was exceptionally short, often only three or four years.

English coach-building was considered to be the best in the world, and many carriage were exported, but a number of them owed both their origin and name to France. The first of these was probably the Omnibus. Another vehicle was the Chaise, which was built to be as comfortable as the chair it represented. Chaise, however, was the word most often used in England when referring to a *Post*-chaise (the carriage used for travel), but there was also a low, four-wheeled vehicle which was known as a pony-chaise.

The two-wheeled Cabriolet, which became so fashionable in London for gentlemen to drive, also originated in France. Another vehicle was the coachman-driven Vis-à-Vis, which although originally made to hold only two people sitting opposite each other was eventually built wider and the name applied to other carriages with similar seating arrangements. Char-à-banc was another carriage whose name remained in England for many years and was even used for motor vehicles made to carry a large number of people.

The Milord also crossed the Channel, although curiously, the name did not remain, for in England it received Royal patronage and it was called a Victoria. Milords were low, open, coach-men driven vehicles which, although fitted with hoods, were more suitable for summer outings. Their counterpart in winter were Coupés—meaning cut—which, since they were shaped like half a coach, described them adequately. Whereas in England these types of carriage were usually known as Broughams,

Left: Travelling in a Calèche with postillion riders.
Left, below: Passengers alighting from a Diligence.
Below: A French Diligence with a pick-axe team driven by a postillion riding the near wheeler.

but were nicknamed 'Growlers' when turned into street cabs, so similarly Coupés, when used for public transport, were re-named 'Fiacres', because they at one time plied for hire outside the Hotel St. Fiacre in Paris.

Three more French vehicles to become popular with the British were the Dormeuse, the Fourgon and the Barouche. The Dormeuse, as its name suggests, was a carriage in which it was possible to lie full length to sleep while travelling, while the Fourgon carried luggage and extra staff. The Barouche was also coachman-driven, but used for grand occasions and was often described as being driven "*à la Daumont*"—which referred to the method of postillion driving made popular by a French nobleman called the Duc d'Aumont. Another coachman-driven vehicle similar to the Barouche was the Calèche, which did not, curiously, reach England, but instead became

Left, above: A Swiss Mail Coach with a pick-axe team—three horses harnessed in front of two wheelers. It can also mean two leaders in front of a single horse.
Left, below: A heavy Belgian horse pulling a mower in the Ardennes.

popular in Germany, where the name of this splendid carriage was spelled Kalesch.

Although the word 'Diligence' occurred occasionally in the English language, the vehicle to which it refers was a French staging coach of considerably bigger proportions than its British counterpart, which never appears to have crossed the Channel. Some of the horses used for pulling Diligences, notably those of the Percheron breed, did however come to England where they proved very popular, particularly for work on the land.

Dutch horses too were at one time very well known

80

in England, as those of the impressive black Friesian breed used to be imported in large numbers for funeral work. In Holland they were and still are extensively used for all types of farm work, and when mares are employed both their yearlings and foals run free beside them, to accustom them to the idea of vehicles and harness. It is traditional, too, for Dutch farmers and their wives to don national costume on festival days and to parade through the streets, driving their Friesian horses to old fashioned chaises. These are high two-wheeled gigs with ogée shaped bodies, with painted panels, decorated by ornate gilded carvings, while the shafts and wheels are white. These vehicles can also be drawn by a pair of horses—the shafts being replaced by a pole while the harness involved resembles that used with Cape Carts in South Africa, which were introduced out there by the Dutch. Another well-known breed of harness horse in Holland is the Gelderland. These are bred in chestnut, bay and grey, and are impressive movers as well as being useful on the land. A third and heavier type of horse is the Groningen, but these are gradually becoming extinct.

Lipizzaners, Kladrubers and Haflingers are the harness breeds to be found in Czechoslovakia and Austria, and Kladrubers which are usually black or grey were considered to have been the classical coach horses. A team of blacks was used for drawing the hearse of the late Emperor Franz-Joseph in Vienna. While Lipizzaners and Kladrubers were in use for carriage work, as well as on the land, the smaller and sturdy Haflingers, which originated in the South Tirol of Austria, were found to be excellent as mountain pack-ponies and useful for pulling carts and sleighs. Their chestnut coats with flaxen manes and tails gave them an attractive appearance, although it was unkindly said that they looked *"a prince in front, a peasant behind."*

Austria also produced a carriage which was introduced into England in 1818. This was the Britchka which, like the French Dormeuse, was a carriage in which it was possible to lie full length. Its unusualness lay in the fact that the bottom of the body was completely flat and that the hood which, when not required, could be folded back.

Although primarily bred in Norway, the Fjord pony soon infiltrated into Denmark where it was used for farm work by small-holders. Like the Haflingers, Fjord ponies are strong and sturdy and possessors of dominant and unusual colouring—their coats are dun-coloured, with black points and dorsal stripes, while their tails and manes are a mixture of silver and black hairs clipped to stand up stiffly to outline the white hair with black. For use with these ponies, Norway produced its own and individual vehicle, one of which is reported to have been brought to England. This was called the Carriole and is described as resembling a sledge on wheels. There were no springs, but the length of the shafts apparently rendered them unnecessary. The harness used with this vehicle is reported as having been very heavy and with enormously

high points to the hames on the collar, which were made of wood. Other breeds in Norway were the Döle Trotters, which are used for harness racing, and the Döle Gudbrandsdal, which are far heavier and resemble English Fell ponies.

As well as the Fjord ponies from neighbouring Norway, Denmark has its own breeds of draught horses. First of these is the chesnut Frederiksborg, which is reputed to have been established since 1562, and is a strong cob with a lot of action. The Jutland horse is considerably bigger and popularised by the well-known Danish breweries. A third breed, the Knabstrup, is an unusual looking spotted horse, many of which were favoured by circus companies.

In Denmark there were a wide selection of carriages, many of them surprisingly having been made by Henry Fife, a coachbuilder who originated from Scotland. The Danish Mail-coach was of unique design in that the body, in which the mails were stored, was spherical, so that it resembled a large pumpkin on wheels and no passengers could be carried.

From Germany an exceedingly popular coachman-driven vehicle was imported into England. This was the Landau, which originated from the town of that name,

A troika team in full flight in Russia. The harness used with troikas is traditionally gay and colourful and includes a high wooden arch called a 'Douga'.

82

A load of timber on a sledge in the forests of Finland.

A siesta for horse and cabby in a cobbled street in Moscow.

where a smaller version, known as the Landaulet, holding only two passengers, was made. Another carriage to bear the name of its town of origin was the Berlin, which was a state coach with a box-seat covered by a hammer-cloth, while the Halberline was, as its name suggests, a smaller version, resembling a chariot. Many other carriages were produced, but it was more for horse breeding that Germany was to become known.

Hanoverian horses first became famous in England when they were imported into the Royal Mews by George Ist. Elsewhere, the lighter Holsteins were popular, as were those of the Oldenburg breed, as well as the Trakehner. The Trakehner has a great reputation for fortitude, for when East Prussia was overrun in 1945 the in-foal mares of this breed were harnessed to wagons and driven 900 miles to safety. Apart from breeding, however, the Germans also became famous for their driving, and trams comprising ten or twelve-in-hands of stallions are regular features at shows organised by the state-owned studs.

Poland also has its individual breeds, among them the Sokólsk and Masuren, while Polish Arabs and Anglo-Arabs are world renowned, the latter being driven as five-in-hands to small vehicles in the same manner as the Hungarians. In Yugoslavia they drive similarly, but use Lipizzaners, which are also found to be useful for farming purposes.

While Switzerland is known mostly for all types of sledges and sleighs, which are drawn by horses wearing colourful harnesses adorned with bells—and these are still used in the winter resorts—two thrilling types of sport have been evolved, one of which consists of harness racing on snow with specially designed sledges, while the other is similar, except that the drivers do not have the advantage of sitting down, but are on skis behind the horses. Known as Skijöering, these unusual methods of harness racing make an exciting spectacle.

Russia is yet another country associated with sleighs and two vehicles as well as a unique style of driving originated there. The Droitska was one carriage, and not unlike the English Victoria in appearance, while the word Troika, although often associated with a vehicle, is a method of driving three horses abreast which was used for both sleighs and wheeled vehicles alike. For this it was essential for the central horse, known as the Korienik, to be both a fast trotter and larger than his companions who, because their heads were pulled permanently to the outside by means of side-straps, were forced to gallop in order to keep up with the trotter.

The harness used with Troikas is traditionally gay and colourful and consists of a high wooden arch called the 'Douga' which is attached to the ends of the shafts and over the middle horse's neck, on which are hung bells and other ornaments. Troika driving was always popular at the time of Imperial Russia, and races are now a feature at the Moscow Hippodrome, together with teams of four horses galloping abreast, which are known as the Tatchanka.

Another Russian vehicle was the Droshki, which is described as having a central and upholstered seat on which two people sat astride, one behind the other. This design was also used for sleighs. In many Scandinavian countries, vehicles had interchangeable undercarriages, so that they could be used on snow and dry land.

In the Southern Hemisphere

NO DOMESTIC OR TRANSPORT animals were indigenous to Australia so in the early days when the idea of exploring the outback first began, all known types of animal were imported and tried. On these journeys, which involved battling with severe climatic adversities, all were found to be wanting: the ox could stand privation and thirst better than the horse, and in the long run provided a better meal—which was the eventual unhappy fate of most transport animals—but he was in general considered to be too slow. Camels, which were introduced from India, could stand the climate and bad conditions better than oxen or horses, but because of their enigmatic natures they required their own specialised handlers who had no desire to explore.

Curiously, the mule, whose hardiness and tenacity might have produced the best of both worlds, was never seriously considered, perhaps because no one had thought of importing the necessary donkeys in order to breed them. It was the horse, therefore, which was eventually selected as the principal beast of burden, and provided water was available horses flourished in the Australian climate. It was, however, many years before bullock wagons, which were unrivalled over very rough country, were superseded, and some continued to haul the heavy loads of wool to railheads right up to the coming of mechanical transport.

From the thoroughbred stock and Cleveland Bays which were imported into Australia during the early part of the 19th Century, a type of light horse was developed. This was to become the standard utility animal in Australia, known for its stamina and suitability for work as a drover's horse, for harness, or indeed as a Cavalry charger. Since they were originally bred in New South Wales, these horses became known as Walers, and large quantities of them were exported to India for use as Army remounts and other work. Apart from Walers a number of heavier draught horses were bred from the original stock of Clydesdales which were imported during the mid-19th Century, and these competed with bullocks for work on farms and for heavy transport in towns. Teams of as many as twenty-six of these horses were used for hauling the huge loads of wool clips.

A type of Stage wagon had been evolved as early as 1814, which was followed in 1821 by a Stage coach, but it was not until the time of the gold rush that a rapidly growing demand for public transport quickly resulted in

Pitt Street, Sydney, about 1890, which has subsequently been destroyed by fire.

Americans, Freeman Cobb, John Murray Peck, James Swanton and J.B. Lamber came to Victoria and imported Concord coaches from the United States. The venture was immediately successful and the famous firm of Cobb and Co. was founded. These coaches were ideally suited to rough going, and at first operated between Melbourne and the Bendigo gold mines, but before long the coaches of Cobb and Co. were in operation over the whole of New South Wales and Queensland, a distance of over 6,000 miles.

Cobb and Co. then set up a coach-building factory at Bathurst, New South Wales, and this was followed by another at Brisbane, Queensland. In 1886 they transferred their factories to Charleville, Queensland, where they constructed coaches to their own design. These closely followed the American coach, but with a few differences, mostly with a view towards cutting costs. The result was a more flat-sided and rectangular coach than the Concord, with none of the refinements such as doors or glass in the windows. Most of these coaches carried fourteen passengers—nine inside and five on top—but some models were made smaller and accommodated only eight people —four inside and four out. These coaches were normally pulled by teams of six horses, but occasionally five or seven were used, which involved three abreast in the lead, with either one pair or two pairs behind them, respectively.

A special type of coach horse was bred—sturdier than the Waler, yet not as heavy as those of the Clydesdale cross—and these were matched as closely as possible in size and pace, and for some of the more important routes, in colour as well. In 1870, over 6,000 horses were covering 28,000 miles a week, and by 1900 nearly all areas in Australia were served by coaches, but with the outbreak of war in 1914 these began to dwindle in numbers and by 1924 the industry had virtually come to a halt.

Apart from the coaching industry in Australia, the building of carriages for private use was also a flourishing concern. In country districts, these often consisted of four-wheeled buggies similar to those used in America, which were suitable for covering rough roads and ground. In the towns more elegant designs built to English patterns were used and with correspondingly smart harness horses pulling them. Many of the English breeds of pony were imported, some of which were excellent for driving privately, for pleasure and sport. Another form of driving, that of harness racing, became immensely popular and in 1869 the Standardbred 'Daniel Boone' was brought over from America to establish this exciting sport which has retained its popularity with the people right up to the present day.

an organised stage coach system being developed. To begin with, mail and stage coaches were imported from England, but it was soon found that these vehicles, which were ideal for fast travelling on good roads, were not suitable for those of the outback. In 1853, four young

Left, above: Carting hay in the mid-northern agricultural area of South Australia.
Far left: Transporting wool bales with up to twelve horses in Australia.
Left: Eight and twelve horse teams sowing wheat in the Wimmera wheat-growing district of Australia.

Top: A Cobb and Co. Coach in difficulty on the road to
Coranderrk near Lilydale, Victoria.
Above: A variation on the Hansom Cab in Melbourne.
Right: A bush scene on the road to Rotomahana, New Zealand.

New Zealand

The early settlers in New Zealand, like those of Australia, had to import animals for transport purposes, since none existed in the country, and it is recorded that the first consignment, which consisted of only three horses, arrived there in December 1814. It was soon found that both the climate and the country were ideal for horses and so many more were imported from Australia, with the result that before long, studs were springing up all over the country.

From the various strains imported, which included Thoroughbred and Arabian horses, a type of native pony was produced which, while ideal for riding and for rounding up cattle, was neither big nor strong enough for heavy draught purposes. Clydesdales were selected and found to be the most suitable breed, both for farm work as well as for crossing with smaller horses to produce sturdy little cobs which were dual purpose—they could be ridden as well as driven. All types of vehicles were imported as well as built in New Zealand—a number of them constructed on American lines.

As was the case in many other countries, harness racing became a major sport, and the first Standardbred horses were brought over from America in 1882. These, like the Clydesdales, Arabs, Thoroughbreds and various English pony breeds, as well as Quarter horses from America, have made New Zealand famous for horse breeding.

South Africa

The climate of Africa is not in general suitable for horses, and in the many large areas inhabited by the Tsetse Fly they are subject to the serious disease known as horse sickness. In *South* Africa, however, horses can exist happily and the early pioneers from Holland soon introduced horses for riding purposes. Dutch farmers much preferred the ox as a transport animal, and it was bullock wagons, rather than horse-drawn vehicles, which predominated in the great trek to the Transvaal and Orange Free State.

The Dutch influence in South Africa produced one very interesting horse-drawn vehicle which was known as the Cape Cart. This was one of the very few two-wheeled vehicles to be drawn by a pair of horses, and the method of draught was the same as that used with gigs in Holland, but different from that for a Curricle (the only other type of two-wheeled horse-drawn carriage which had a bar fitted across the horses' backs to support the weight of the pole) in that the pole of a Cape Cart was attached to a long wooden bar which was held up by straps round the horses' necks. Cape Carts were fitted with canvas hoods with folding glass shutters which could be drawn across the front. These contained a small window through which the occupant could drive or, if required, the vehicle could be completely enclosed and driven by a native boy perched on a small saddle behind

the footboard. The latter method was obviously favoured during the dry season, when dust was a problem.

At one time the mails were carried in two-wheeled carts, although by 1870 Freeman Cobb, one of the American founders of the famous firm of Cobb and Co.'s coaches in Australia, decided, perhaps in view of the discovery of diamonds in South Africa, to try his hand at building up yet another coaching concern. With a friend, he imported six Concord coaches from America and announced that these would run between Port Elizabeth and the diamond mines at New Rush. As had been the case in Australia, the same careful planning of stages and accommodation for passengers was worked out, but the venture, due to bad roads, expensive fodder and, even worse, horse sickness was not a success and after four years the company went into liquidation. Freeman Cobb died at the early age of 46.

Meanwhile, an Englishman, John Alexander Gibson, who had had coaching experience in England, decided to go into the transport business with his brother, and their first company, the Red Star Line, which was run on the same lines as those of Cobb and Co. and also with Concord coaches, was an immediate success. By this time the railways were infiltrating into South Africa, although coaches were still found to be useful in linking the rail heads with the diamond mines, and when gold was discovered this brought an even greater number of people to require coach services. In addition to the Gibsons' successful Red Star Line coaches, other proprietors soon set up rival concerns—among them the Swedish Zeederburg brothers, who were asked by Cecil Rhodes to set up a service to Bulawayo, but this was so far north that it brought serious health problems for the horses, and so mules which were more resistant to disease were tried and imported in large quantities from South America. Following on this, the Zeederburgs attempted mixed teams containing mules and the native zebras, but although the zebras were almost completely resistant to the dreaded horse sickness, their vicious temperaments made them almost impossible to work. Zeederburg coaches were, however, used extensively during the Boer War, and until well into the 20th Century.

Besides these Concord coaches, which were used by Cobb, the Gibsons and the Zeederburg brothers, most other vehicles, like those in Australia, were of American design as it was found that they were better fitted to withstand the rough roads. In the towns, however, lighter carriages of English design made their appearance, together with a number of British born horses and ponies. Apart from Thoroughbreds, which are used for both breeding and racing, Arabian and Welsh pony stock have made their mark on the country. The American Saddlebred is also a popular horse, particularly with the farming community. It has Morgan blood in its ancestry and can be used for riding and all types of harness work.

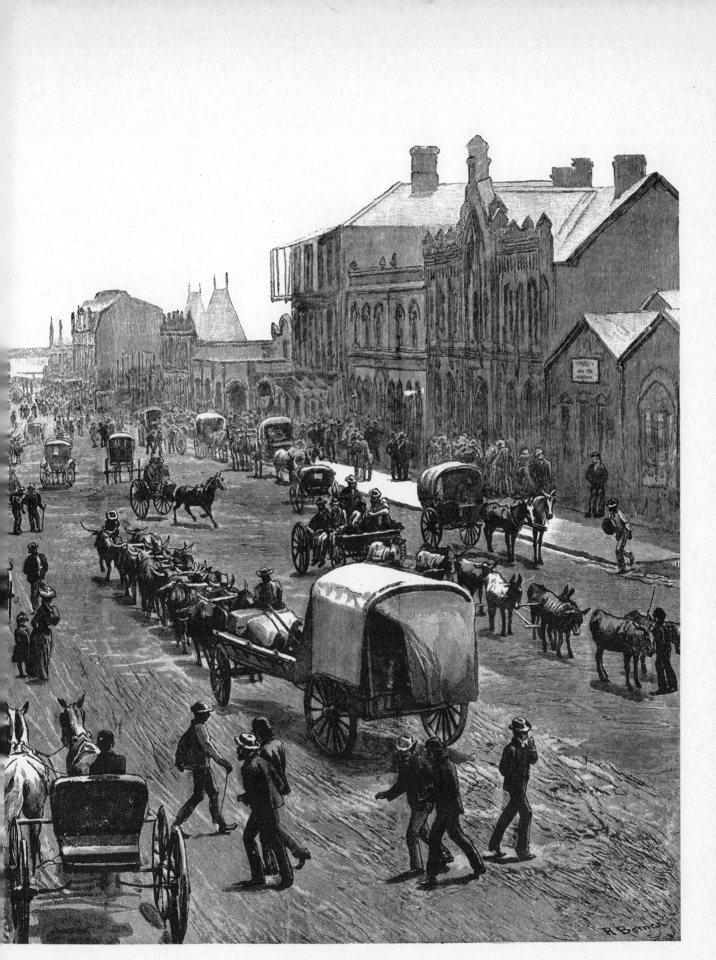

The main street in Johannesburg, South Africa, about 1891.

India

In the plains of India, large wooden wagons drawn by either oxen or ponderous black water buffaloes have always been used for agriculture and the transport of heavy goods, but for journeys to and around the bazaars, towns and villages there were several types of horse-drawn vehicles. First, and the most primitive, was the Ekka—the name being believed to have evolved from Hackney which, in its turn came from the French 'Haquenée', meaning a horse for hire.

The construction of an Ekka was that of a small square platform on two wheels, surmounted by a fringed and curtained canopy supported by four poles, and although the space on them was extremely limited, Ekkas were frequently crammed with passengers who clung both to each other as well as the canopy poles for support, while if need be the driver sat over the side or even upon a shaft. The ponies used for drawing these vehicles were small, thin countrybreds, many of them entires. However, in spite of their heavy loads, or perhaps more on account of the use of the whip, Ekka ponies usually managed to keep up a fast trot.

The second and higher grade of vehicle for hire was the Tonga. Throughout the years the design of Tongas appears to have altered, or perhaps it might be more accurate to say that the name Tonga has been applied to different vehicles, for according to both an early photo-graph, as well as to a description in an Army manual, the Tonga was at one time a low, hooded and clumsily built vehicle on two wheels, which was drawn by a pair harnessed 'curricle fashion'—with a bar across their backs to support the weight of the pole between them. Another description, as well as a drawing by the late Lord Baden-Powell in his book "*Indian Memories*", shows it as having shafts with one pony, while another was hitched along-side in what he describes as 'Hungarian' fashion. In later years the vehicle known as a Tonga was drawn by a single horse only, and in design resembled an English Ralli car, with the driver and passengers sitting back to back under a fringed canopy.

Tongas were used by a great many people since they were considered of a higher social grade than Ekkas and more comfortable to travel in. They were far easier to enter, for there was a low foot-board at the back. The ponies drawing Tongas were, like those in Ekkas, fre-quently country-bred, and some of them had formerly been used for playing Polo.

A third type of vehicle was the dark and gloomy Bhund, or closed gharry, which was a square box-like carriage on four wheels, with shutters instead of windows which gave it the appearance of a Black Maria. Bhund gharries were used for transporting families and luggage, but they also carried an air of mystery, since Indian ladies in purdah could sometimes be glimpsed peeping from within.

There is no doubt but that the arrival of the British in India contributed largely to the design of other vehicles, the 'Fitton' gharry for instance. These were Victorias with four wheels covered by sweeping mudguards and driven from a box-seat. Fitton gharries, the name most probably being derived from phaeton, began as the property of higher class people, but when shabby and discarded were used, like so many of their kind all over the world, to ply for hire. As in England, smaller vehicles such as two-wheeled gigs were found to be extremely useful for people wishing to drive themselves. These were always known as 'Tum-Tums'—the word being perhaps derived from Tandem, since some early sportsmen probably used them for driving horses in this fashion.

Tum-Tums were built on the lines of a Cabriolet, hooded and with a small platform at the back on which the 'syce' or native groom, sat while his English counter-part used this for standing on. They were driven by most British residents, while the horses were also used for hack-ing or for playing polo.

For ceremonial and Vice-Regal occasions open Land-aus and Barouches from England were used, drawn by pairs of horses driven postillion, and with out-riders. The native ponies were too small for these vehicles and so the Australian breed of Walers, which had been imported for the use of the Army and the Police, were found to be ideal as carriage horses, since they stood about 16-hands and had a great deal of both presence and bone. Some wealthy Indians and those of the ruling classes took great pride in

Left: Driving a 'Fitton' gharry in the monsoon in Bombay.
Above: An Indian Tonga in dire trouble on a mountain road.
Below: An early print of an Indian Ekka.

their carriages, importing all types from England and evolving splendidly coloured liveries for their staff. Lord Baden-Powell describes a journey made in a Rajah's elegant barouche which was drawn by two white horses whose tails had been dyed a brilliant pink to match the coats and puggaries of the driver and syces!

Most of the country-bred horses were small and with little bone, although those from the Northern parts of India were frequently larger and with more substance. Like many other countries, Arab horses were imported and used extensively for cross-breeding which, with both Waler and Thoroughbred blood, produced good animals for both riding and harness.

WITH THE DAWN OF THE 20TH Century, the use of horse power began to decline, but the interest in coaching which had been revived in the 1860s by the Duke of Beaufort remained. Stage coaches were resuscitated and many an old route re-opened. The year 1888 saw an historic run performed by Jim Selby when, for a wager of £1,000, he drove the 'Old Times' coach from London to Brighton and back—a distance of 108 miles—in under eight hours. A record was also achieved at one of the many stops, when his ostlers changed a team of horses in 47 seconds, though this was beaten at the 1963 International Horse Show, when the grooms to the 'Red Rover' coach achieved a time of 45 seconds!

Another sportsman was the Earl of Lonsdale who, in

Below: H.R.H. The Princess Anne leaving Buckingham Palace for Westminster Abbey, on the occasion of her marriage to Captain Mark Phillips, in November 1973.

1891, drove twenty miles in four five-mile laps, with four different methods of driving in under one hour. The enthusiasm for driving was not, however, limited to the English. Mr. Alfred Vanderbilt was one of many Americans to drive, and between 1908 and 1914 his 'Viking' and 'Venture' coaches and teams of greys which he had shipped from the States became well known on the London to Brighton road during the summer months.

Between the two great world wars, driving in England still flourished, albeit on a small scale, and the Coaching Club which had been formed in 1871 was still in existence and holding regular meets in Hyde Park. Few people imagined that it would, or could, survive the Second World War, yet the driving of horses still held its magic. Gigs, Dog-carts and Phaetons which had almost been relegated to the scrap-heap were brought out. Coaches were repainted and horses broken to harness. Several long distance journeys have been achieved, including Edinburgh to London, and the roads from London to Southampton and Brighton were covered by the 'Red Rover' coach.

By far the most ambitious journey was the "*Tulip run*"

made in 1960 by Mr. Van der Touw of Holland. He drove his coach from Istanbul to Rotterdam, a distance of about 2,175 miles, in thirty-nine days. A more recent run took place in the USA when Mr. P. B. Hofmann faced the New York traffic to drive to Philadelphia.

The enthusiasm for driving in England produced the British Driving Society, which was formed in 1956 to ensure that both the history and art of driving should not be lost to posterity, and from a small beginning, the Society grew. Lectures, demonstrations and rallies which are held throughout Britain have inspired similar organisations overseas. By far the most impressive development in driving has, however, been provided by the Duke of Edinburgh when, under his Chairmanship, the FEI (Fédération Equestre Internationale) adopted rules for competitions similar to those held for Equestrian events. For pairs and four-in-hands, these involve: Presentation; Dressage; Cross-country and Obstacle driving at which His Royal Highness is himself no mean exponent. Teams from Great Britain have so far been successful in these competitions both at home as well as abroad.

Top: H.R.H. The Duke of Edinburgh driving a four-in-hand at the Royal Windsor Horse Show.
Above: Mr. Sanders Watney, The President of the British Driving Society, driving a tandem.

Index

The numbers in italic refer to illustrations.

96